EVERYTHING YOU ~~EVER WANTED TO KNOW~~ ABOUT KEANU

His Childhood . . .

Learn the truth about his constantly uprooted early years, and how his life with his costume-designing mother led him to pal around with the likes of Alice Cooper as a child.

His Vagabond Lifestyle . . .

Keanu prefers the bohemian life, riding his motorcycle, playing in his band, and living in a hotel rather than buying a house he can well afford. Learn his secret for staying so detached from Hollywood, and from life in general. What will make this wandering heartthrob settle down?

His Passion for Acting . . .

The huge success of *Speed* rocketed Keanu to stardom, but his true passion remains Shakespeare.

KEANU REEVES

CHRIS NICKSON

St. Martin's Paperbacks

KEANU REEVES

Copyright © 1996 by Chris Nickson.

Cover photograph courtesy Sygma.

ISBN: 0-312-95885-4

Printed in the United States of America

St. Martin's Paperbacks edition / August 1996

10 9 8 7 6 5 4 3 2 1

This book is for my nephews—Greg Stuart Nickson and Wesley Jacob Nagel. Live long and prosper.

Acknowledgments

To begin, many, many thanks to Madeleine Morel, a true goddess among agents. And also to John Rounds, a prince among editors, who thought my idea had merit.

Writing this book would have been infinitely harder without the help and signposts of the following articles: "Peaking In The Valley" by Lynn Snowden, in *Rolling Stone*, March 9, 1989, the Keanu Reeves interview in *US* from March 1995, Lyle Slack's profile "Keanu's Excellent Adventure" in *Maclean's*, January 23, 1995, "Goodbye, Airhead" by David Ansen in *Newsweek*, June 13, 1994, *Vanity Fair*'s cover story, "The Wild One," by Michael Shnayerson in August 1995, and the features in *People*, "If You Knew Keanu . . . You'd Be Rare" (July 11, 1994), "Fresh Prince" (February 6, 1995), and "Much Ado About Keanu" (June 5, 1995).

And, of course, it's impossible to forget Ray and Betty Nickson, Bob and Florence Hornberg, the Nagels (now a happy threesome), and Watkins, who continually offer encouragement, as do a wide range of friends—Dave, Dennis, Mike, Dani, Kevin. You know who you are. I'm grateful to you all.

I doubt whether much of this would have been possible without the support of Linda, who while pregnant and with plenty to think about, was happy to let me burble out my news, ideas, and theories. I love you very, very much.

INTRODUCTION

To call Keanu Reeves one of today's hottest tickets might be something of an understatement. Along with Tom Cruise and Brad Pitt, he's become one of Hollywood's three biggest leading men, a real superstar. *Bill and Ted's Excellent Adventure* established him, *Point Break* cemented his status, and three years later, *Speed* sent him into the stratosphere.

He's gone from airhead to hustler to action hero to cyberpunk and romantic dreamer, finding time along the way to squeeze in the Buddha and a vampire killer. As film careers go, his has been remarkably varied.

And as the journey progressed he managed to become a real movie star, a pinup and sex symbol to people around the globe. Teen magazines call him one of the "hot babes," along with faces like Brad Pitt. It's not a situation he would have ever foretold, and not one he ever went searching for—or even really wanted. But whether he's the goof of *Bill and Ted's Excellent Adventure* or the buff hero of *Speed*, he's managed to strike a very resonant chord in hearts and minds all over the world.

If any one male film star sums up his generation, it's Keanu. He's a chameleon, literally changing physically with each role. In *Little Buddha* his frame was emaciated, making him the perfect ascetic philosopher. When he arrived on the set of *Speed*, a few weeks later, his hair was cut in a very businesslike crop, and his muscles bulged as if he'd been working out for years. He was, in mind and body, already Jack Traven.

As an actor he's managed to be taken very seriously, to the point where he's been offered $10 million dollars to film a sequel to *Speed*, which was a box office smash and one of the top grossing films of 1994.

At the Art Center College of Design in Pasadena, California, they even teach a course about his work. And it's definitely not an easy grade.

* * *

But what about the man himself? He keeps incredibly busy, and is always in demand, virtually moving from film to film without pause. It's as if he has no real life beyond acting. In some ways that's true. Outside his profession, his interests are very few—his motorcycle and his band are about all. Although he's long been able to afford it, he's not interested enough to buy himself a house. So instead he lives in a hotel—although, admittedly, a good one.

Keanu has fallen into his success, and embraced it somewhat warily. It's there, it's happened, but he's not sure he really wants it.

He's certainly not interested in the trappings that accompany fame. If pressed, he'll present an award at the Oscars, but you won't find his face haunting the gossip columns or the tabloids. For one thing, he's too busy most of the time. And when he isn't, he stays well away from that world of roving cameras and reporters out for a story.

He's the bass player for Dogstar, a band he calls "folk-thrash," but which others have labeled rather less kindly. When they perform, though, it's a certainty the venue will be sold out. Mostly, that's people coming to see Keanu, but at least some of them will really listen.

It's his chance to wind down, to escape the pressures of moviemaking. He grew up with music, like the rest of his generation. It's one of the ways he can define who he is. So, like many of his contemporaries, he learned to play an instrument and joined a group.

And when he really wants to get away, he climbs on his only treasured possession, an old 1972 Norton Commando 850 motorcycle, and takes off. Somtimes he does it late at night. With the headlights off. To him there's a big element of fun in the danger.

For someone who seems to have no real ambition about his life beyond acting, events have overtaken him at a rapid rate. He's become one of the most sought-after actors around. As one of the new stars of Hollywood, and a true heartthrob, he could have any number of leading roles.

But all too often, they're not the ones that interest him. So he'll take a smaller, supporting part, something he can work with and enjoy.

He's also virtually the only American film star of his generation to show any real interest in stage work in general, and Shakespeare in particular. It's a challenge, a risk, and it's appealing. So, in January 1995, Keanu found himself freezing in Winnipeg, Canada, while treading the boards as Hamlet. He could have been in a better, more prestigious location, but that wasn't the point. The chance was offered, and he grabbed it. And it certainly didn't stop Keanu fans from any number of countries flying in and paying scalpers exorbitant prices to catch their hero performing in the flesh for three hours.

That is a measure of the man, as well as of the people who idolize him.

For all his remarkable visibility on screen, with twenty-three movies in ten years, there's still plenty about him that's stayed private. He's shied away from the press throughout his career, giving interviews very rarely, and letting his characters be his public face.

With no real home, no real girlfriend, and no solid ground around him except the constantly shifting sets of whatever movie he's filming at the time, he's managed to stay very detatched from life. It's as if he could leave it all behind at any time; start the bike and move on somewhere else.

But at the same time, there's an innocence and openness about him, a vulnerability. People, fans, those who've worked with him—all feel an urge to protect him from life.

"There's a hint of sadness in his eyes," said Sandra Bullock, who co-starred with Keanu in *Speed*.

"It makes you want to go, 'What *is* it?' "

Maybe he doesn't even know what it is himself. Maybe he doesn't really want, or need, to find out. Because without that quality he'd be somebody completely different, less curious, less adventurous. Someone he might not like.

Acting is his joy. That's why he does it. He happens to have a gift for it that has grown into a money-making machine. Keanu Reeves might be a hero for the slacker generation, and he might give the impression that he's one of them, but he's one of the hardest working men in movies. He's driven.

On the set, he's completely professional—always on time and prepared for the day's shooting. It's a complete contrast to the vacant image he's had ever since he became indelibly associated with the character of Ted "Theodore" Logan, hair flopping into his eyes, uttering a selection of cliches and calling everyone dude. He was truly "most excellent" in the part, but that was what it was—a part. It wasn't him.

In real life, Keanu is not an avid conversationalist. But he can speak in a way that, although sometimes a little strange—he'll put in little asides to himself—doesn't depend on platitudes to get by. And, to pass the long hours when he's not needed for filming, he's quite likely to spend the time in his trailer reading Shakespeare. Not exactly the action of an airhead.

He lives completely in the present. Only with regard to his career is there the vaguest planning for the future, and even that only extends to the next year or two. There's no big game plan, no design. On a personal level, beyond playing with Dogstar and riding his motorcycle, well, the future's wide open. It's easier that way, for the moment, anyway.

No ties, plenty of money, fame . . . it seems like an ideal life. And Keanu has no complaints about it. Some astonishment at being a heartthrob, yes. But that's out of his hands, he can't control it. So he doesn't worry about it. His job is to give the best performance he can in every role.

But the fascination people have with him remains, and grows stronger with each film he makes. His unusual, slightly exotic look, his offbeat private life that leaves him slightly unknowable; they're the things that intrigue the fans, and leave them wanting to know more.

So who exactly is this man who has the great film directors, from Bertolucci to Coppola, eager to work with him? What is the magic he possesses that makes him one of the major new stars? Where did he come from, and what brought him to the point he's reached today?

CHAPTER ONE

Before the strife began and it became a city of bombs, mortars, and sniper fire, Beirut was a golden place. With a population of 700,000, the capital of Lebanon was always busy and vital. Since the end of World War II, its reputation had increased to the point where it had become the Middle East's center of commerce and shipping.

The hotels were full of businessmen and tourists. In the suburbs the rich lived in houses that were nothing short of mansions.

The nightlife was legendary. Big names came in to entertain. There was always plenty to do in Beirut. Things to see, places to go. The waters of the Mediterranean, on the beaches away from the docks, were warm and inviting.

In the mid-'60s it seemed like heaven. People came to call it the Paris of the Middle East, and it was an apt nickname. A city of wealth and luxury, Beirut was cosmopolitan, charming.

Certainly Samuel Nowlin Reeves and his wife Patricia (who was also known as Patric) thought so. It suited the way they wanted to live. They weren't among the high rollers, the rich and famous, but Beirut had plenty to offer them anyway.

Samuel Reeves, who was Hawaiian-Chinese, was a geologist, an educated man with good, steady employment. Patricia had been born in England, and studied as a theatrical designer in London.

They'd met in Beirut, where Samuel was working for an oil company, and Patricia, having followed the bohemian trail slowly east, was earning a living as a showgirl in a local nightclub. Friendship turned to love, and soon to marriage. They were able to live very comfortably on the money Samuel was earning, better than either had before, with a spacious house and servants. It seemed close to paradise.

That was where Keanu (the name translates from Hawaiian as "cool breeze over the mountains") Charles Reeves was born on September 2, 1964. His mother's features dominated his face, but there was still a definite touch of his father around the eyes and the cheekbones, enough to make the boy seem exotic.

When he was four, his mother gave birth to another child, a daughter, Kim, and the family seemed complete. But it was time to move on from the Middle East. They'd been there during the Six Day War in 1967, when Israel won an amazing victory over its aggressors. Tensions were rising again. It was better to leave Beirut.

And so they ended up in Australia for a few months before coming to the United States, or more exactly, New York. It seemed an odd place for the family after several years of sun, sand, and relative freedom. And it proved not so much a new beginning as an end.

Samuel and Patricia separated, and divorced soon after. Samuel went back to Hawaii. Patricia stayed where she was.

She didn't really like New York. It didn't strike her a good place to raise kids—there was no garden for them to play in, no real space anywhere. Instead, there was constant traffic, dirt on everything, and noise from all the people.

But it did have culture, museums, and plays. All the bands played there. She came to know people involved with the arts in all forms, and to pay her bills returned to a profession she'd had in England, designing costumes for a wide range of theatrical productions.

Soon she met a director, Paul Aaron, a man who worked both on Broadway and in Hollywood, and in 1970, when Keanu was six, they married. After the ceremony, once they were settled, they talked seriously about moving with the kids. Patricia still didn't like New York. She needed to leave, and the sooner the better. But the suburbs, where most people migrated, weren't any kind of answer; she was far too bohemian to ever fit in there.

Finally they came up with a solution, albeit an unlikely one. Toronto. It was an accessible big city with lots happening, but next to no crime. They could afford a house up there. It had all the advantages of New York and none of the drawbacks. It seemed perfect.

Except for the weather, of course. That was far from ideal, at least for Keanu. The Big Apple had seemed bad enough to him after the desert warmth he'd known. Toronto in the winter might as well have been the North Pole. And all too often it seemed like it was.

He'd developed into a child who'd often drift away, lost in his own thoughts. Patricia would ask him to do something, then return a few minutes later to find him still staring into space. She'd just shake her head and tap him on the shoulder to bring him back to earth.

That dreaminess stayed with him as he started classes at Jesse Ketchum Grade School in downtown Toronto. However well intentioned he was, it seemed that punctuality wasn't going to be among Keanu's virtues.

"I don't think he was ever on time for any lesson," said teacher Paula Warder. But, when he did finally arrive, the happy boy who was usually hidden came out and ". . . he had a smile on his face." But lessons weren't easy for him; Keanu was dyslexic, and although he later overcame the problem, it made school life difficult when he was young.

Although they got along well with their stepfather, Keanu and Kim missed Samuel. That was perfectly understandable and natural. They wanted to see him, but the sheer distance made that difficult. As it was, they were able to travel to Hawaii sometimes during school vacations to spend time with their father. It wasn't the same as being with him regularly, but it was all that was possible.

Keanu treasured the visits. Walking off the plane into a warm day, seeing his father, and talking became the high points in his life. It all lasted until he was thirteen.

They were in Kauai, on the last night of the chil-
drens' visit. Kim was already asleep, and Keanu
and Samuel sat outside, gazing up at the dark sky.
Samuel had seemed different this time. A lot of
what he said made no sense to the boy.

The next day Keanu and Kim flew back to Canada. And nothing more was heard of Samuel
Reeves for ten years. He simply dropped out of
sight. No letters, no calls. The children, even Patricia, had no idea what to think, and, living half a
world away, there was very little they could do.
They called the police; he wasn't in jail, the hospital, or the morgue. He'd just vanished.

The separation and divorce, the visits to his father, his father's disappearance—they all had a
huge effect on Keanu. He felt isolated. He had no
real friends. He blamed it all on his father for leaving. As he said later, "I think a lot of who I am is
a reaction against his actions."

Samuel Reeves did eventually re-emerge after
more than a decade, but there was no communi-
cation between him and his former family. He remained in Hawaii, and in July 1994, he was
sentenced by a court there to ten years in jail for
cocaine possession, lessening the already slim
chances of any late reconciliation with his children.

Keanu's pain remained, sharp and strong.

At home, he got on with his life. By most accounts he was a well-behaved child, who took to building go-carts and enjoying the usual pranks of childhood.

"We did sling chestnuts at teachers' heads," he admitted later. It was all innocent fun, at least until he became a teenager.

". . . in Grade 8 hash started to come around, and LSD kinda."

But by that time, Keanu had developed an obsession with sports, and in particular that most Canadian game, ice hockey.

"Keanu was major hockey," Paul Aaron recalled in *Maclean's*. "That's all he talked about, thought about."

There was no shortage of rinks where he could practice. Keanu wasn't big—wiry would be the best description—which made things difficult for him, but he soon found a home for himself as a goalie, where it wasn't so much his size, but his speed, skill, and courage that were tested.

Perhaps surprisingly, the boy who'd spent his first few years playing in the sand proved to be perfectly at ease on the ice, becoming quite accomplished in his position. Like almost every other boy in Canada, he began to dream of playing professional hockey.

And he came closer than most. While he was a student at De La Salle College, a Catholic high school in Toronto, he played goalie for their hockey team, ending the season as their most valuable player, with the nickname of "The Wall" for his strong defense. Those were high accolades, and for a while his dream of playing for the Maple Leafs seemed a little closer.

At home things stayed in a constant state of flux. The marriage between Patricia and Paul Aaron lasted only a year, although the friendship remained solid, and Aaron stayed an important figure in Keanu's life. Soon Patricia wed again, to Robert Miller, a promoter of rock'n'roll shows in the city, and with him she gave birth to another child, a daughter they named Karina. She'd also gone back to plying her trade as a costume designer, making her own income. There were plenty of theaters in Toronto, and work came in, but she started to set her sights on more distant horizons. She loved music, and kept records playing all the time she was sewing at home. She could see that the stage acts of many of the new bands were becoming more theatrical. If she could start designing and making costumes for them, who could tell, there might be plenty of money in that. Even more, it would open up a whole new social world. Actors were fine, often funny, and she'd met quite a few of them through Paul. But musicians, well, that would be hip.

The little brick house in Yorkville, Toronto's hippie section, seemed so normal on the outside, with its garage and small backyard where the wading pool stayed full all summer. But soon vans were pulling up, and bizarrely dressed, long-haired men were knocking on the door and disappearing inside.

Real rock stars dropped by and sometimes stayed for a few days. Patricia was doing work for Dolly Parton. And what thirteen year old wouldn't have relished the idea of David Bowie or Alice Cooper as a houseguest?

"I remember [Alice] brought fake vomit and dog pooh to terrorize the housekeeper," Keanu recalled. "He'd hang out, a regular dude. A friend of mine and I, you know, wrestled with him once . . ."

If it was a slightly odd existence for two kids growing up, it was also a happy one, unconventional but plenty of fun. Halloween was always extravagant, with wonderful costumes for Keanu to wear—Dracula, Batman (with his younger sister as Robin), and Cousin It from *The Addams Family*.

It didn't get much better than that, really. Home had become a giant playground. Keanu and Kim never knew quite what they'd find when they got home from school.

Much of the time Keanu was left to his own devices. He didn't talk much about his real father.

"If he ever came up in conversation, Keanu would change the subject," said Shawn Aberle, a childhood friend. "He felt a little bit alone."

Sometimes, during vacations, Keanu would fly off to spend time with Paul Aaron and visit the set of whatever project he was working on at the time. Usually, he was in Hollywood, working on films like *A Different Story*, *Force of One*, and a remake of *The Miracle Worker* for NBC television, which won an Emmy.

Between the work his mother did and the people who visited the house, the kids found themselves surrounded by arty people. Keanu didn't have too many friends his own age, so he tended to spend most of his free time at home, either alone in his room, or just hanging out with his mother and her friends, who took the relaxed, easygoing kid in easily, treating him like an adult. He went with them to concerts, everything from the metal of Alice Cooper to the country of Emmylou Harris, reveling in the open acceptance. It wasn't the same as having good, close buddies, but at the time it seemed like a very acceptable substitute.

* * *

Like almost every teenager, Keanu's interests changed regularly. Even so, and despite his having time on movie sets with Paul, it was still a surprise to Patricia when the confirmed jock expressed an interest in acting. It didn't really seem like his sort of thing at all. And he certainly had no idea it would change his life. But when the notices went up about auditions for the school play—a production of *The Crucible*, Arthur Miller's drama about witch burning—Keanu decided to try out for a part.

To his surprise, he was given one. To his even greater astonishment, he liked it and was good in the role. Not outstanding, but it was very early days yet. And he elicited a reaction from the audience, even if it wasn't one he'd expected.

Patricia was there to see her son's opening night. She wouldn't have missed it. As he stood onstage asking, "What am I?" she heard the dreamy whisper of a girl from the row behind her, "A hunk." It was a shock. This was her son. She'd never considered that someone would think of him like that.

From that point Keanu was sold on the idea of being an actor. His performance might have been ragged, but just doing it, being up on stage bringing a character to life, felt right. It felt like the thing he wanted to do with his life. He didn't completely abandon hockey, but now it took a back seat, along with everything else, to this new interest.

Patricia wasn't too shocked, then, when Keanu announced that he wanted to audition for a place at Toronto's new High School for the Performing Arts. She was a little concerned, though. Even at the Catholic high school, which had been his third, he hadn't settled. Why would this be any different?

But he managed to persuade her to at least let him try out. Everything seemed to weigh against him. He was a newcomer to stage work, a real novice with just one production to his credit. He had no grasp of technique or style. He was competing against kids with plenty of experience for the twenty-five available places. But the teachers saw something in him. Against all odds, he was offered a place.

"Then, like everything else he does, that became his sole abiding interest," Aaron recalled. "I mean, every part of it—the voice, the movement, the contemporary, the classical."

While he was a student there, he took advantage of every opportunity to work. At sixteen, he tried out to appear in a Canadian television commerical for Coca-Cola. If he got the part, he'd have to appear as a racing cyclist. He appeared at the office of agent Tracy Moore, who was representing him, proud to show off his legs, which he'd shaved to imitate real cyclists. He was naive, but undeniably enthusiastic. And he did end up being cast in the commercial, which was shown across the country. It was his first television appearance.

But not his last, however. It wouldn't be too long before he was finding walk-on roles in a few Canadian series, like the "tall villain" in the crime show *Night Heat*. Anyone could have blinked and missed him, but it was a start, another line for his resume.

Acting consumed him. It was his be all and end all. Unfortunately, that concentration didn't always extend to other parts of the work. He'd turn up for auditions in dress pants chopped down to shorts. Sometimes he'd even forget to shower—although directors would invariably remind him of the fact. The way he dressed or smelled was irrelevant to him. It had nothing to do with the part. More than once Moore had to take him in hand.

"We didn't want him to be remembered as a sloppy, smelly kid," Moore said later, "but his attitude was, that didn't have anything to do with acting ability."

And his total concentration and dedication to his craft created problems at school. The school might have catered to the artistically gifted, but there was still an academic curriculum to be followed—and passed. That was the trouble. Keanu just couldn't pass. He even repeated a year, and yet again, failed everything.

"I even flunked gym," he said.

He wanted to act. School was good, very useful, but he couldn't stay there anymore. He had gotten everything he could from the place. So after talking with his mother, he decided to drop out at the age of seventeen, one credit short of graduation. It was a solution of sorts, but it raised a big question—what was he going to do now?

He already knew the answer. Act. He needed more training first, he knew that. So he auditioned to enter the acting school at Leah Posluns, a community theater located in suburban Toronto.

When he arrived for his tryout dressed in torn jeans and unlaced sneakers with hair hanging over his face, no one was impressed, especially Rose Dubin, who directed the school. Once Keanu began his monologue, though, ". . . we just sat there and he blew us away," she recalled. "He had such energy. Goofy and sort of macho and sort of uncertain. On the threshold of growing up but not quite there."

Needless to say, his performance guaranteed him

a place at the school. When he began, the other students had no idea what to make of him.

"I thought he was kind of an idiot at first," one said.

He might have been lacking in the technical skills and raw in his presentation, but he had an actor's instincts and emotions.

"It was straight from the heart," the student continued. "He didn't really know what he was doing—but he knew what to do, if that makes any sense . . . people seemed to like it."

He learned a lot at Leah Posluns—how to breathe, how to stand, the "Method" for projecting himself into the characters he was playing. They taught all the aspects of acting technique, and Keanu just drank it all in. He was like a sponge, absorbing the words and figuring out how to apply them to his work.

After school he worked at small jobs that would bring him money—trimming trees or sharpening ice skates.

Another passion also began to enter his life now. Music. It had always been around him, virtually as far back as he could remember. But that had been Patricia's music. It had been cool, but it wasn't his. Now, a few years late, he discovered punk rock, something his mother didn't enjoy, something that could be *his*.

A punk scene had sprung up in Toronto in some of the small clubs. People wore strange clothes and had their hair cut in bizarre styles. At seventeen Keanu was strictly too young to be there (the drinking age is nineteen in Canada), but was able to fake his way in. Most of the major bands, both from Britain and the U.S., came through town, so he had plenty of opportunity to see the new heroes who were changing the face of music.

And, finally, he gained freedom of a sort. As soon as he'd saved enough money from work, he bought a car from an old family friend. It wasn't anything extravagant, just a 1969 Volvo 122. The front seat was held up with bricks, which made sudden stops a little dangerous. But the car had two things going for it: it was painted British racing green, which made it look fast even if it wasn't, and it had a great stereo.

So now Keanu could rattle around the city, the Clash blasting out of the tape deck. He found a new job, one that offered plenty of flexibility—delivering pasta for a store called Pastissima. Whenever he had an audition, he wasn't available; it was a simple as that.

He had a car and money. Life was getting better.

And more adventurous. One night he and a few friends drove from Toronto to Buffalo, New York, to catch a performance by The Ramones, one of the first American punk bands.

"... all those questions that run through your head: 'Will we make it?' 'Yes, of course.' 'We're under age. Can we get it?' 'Yeah, cool.'"

They did get in, faking their way past the doorman. It was the first real road trip. But there'd be a much bigger one coming.

In the spring of 1984, he made his professional stage debut in *Wolfboy*, which was staged by the Theatre Passe Muraille in Toronto. At first, though, it didn't seem that he was going to land the part. John Palmer, the play's director, wasn't impressed by Keanu's audition. And, to be fair, he still had a long way to go; his training had just begun, and his technique was still being formed. What he did have on his side, Palmer recalled, was "an energy and a glow" that would capture an audience.

And he did. As the lead, he played a disturbed youth, who was committed to a psychiatric hospital and who fell under the spell of another patient—a boy who ended up sucking his blood in a vampire's manner. The play became a cult hit in the city, resonating strongly with the gay community in the early days of AIDS deaths. With its success, Keanu acquired his first gay following, one which would increase seven years later when he starred in *My Own Private Idaho*.

Meanwhile, acting just kept on becoming a bigger part of Keanu's life. Most evenings he was out, either at class or rehearsing a play. He was putting more energy into his new craft than he'd ever mustered for school, and it was definitely beginning to pay off. His technique was improving. It was exciting. He was even coming to appreciate Shakespeare, something none of his English teachers had ever managed to inspire in him. Spoken aloud, on a stage, the language had a rare beauty and power. And, he realized, once you knew what was going on, they were great stories. It was the way drama should be.

He still shot baskets for fun and played ice hockey, but the dreams he'd had about turning professional were long gone. These days, acting was the only thing he could really imagine doing for a living.

Keanu's work in *Wolfboy* had gotten him noticed. He still wasn't the smoothest, or even the most accomplished performer at Leah Posluns, but he had *something*, a passion, an indefinable star quality that made him instantly memorable and charismatic on stage. More television work began coming his way. He changed agents, signing with Lisa Burke, who specialized in the field.

However, the sudden success and adulation seemed to go to his head a little. Before long, directors were complaining to Burke about Keanu. He was unprofessional. He'd show up late, or he'd think he knew better than everyone else and refuse to take direction. It was worrying for her. Finally she gave Keanu an ultimatum.

"The substance was either shape up or ship out," she remembered. "Slowly, I think, he began to realize he loved this business and started taking it seriously. From there on everything was fine."

Once that was settled, and Keanu understood that there were plenty of other talented individuals out there eager to take his place, he calmed down, at least until the word came through that he'd won a place to study at the Hedgerow Theater in Pennsylvania for the summer. With plenty of work and now this, he could have been forgiven if he'd believed himself one of Toronto's hottest young actors.

It was his first real trip away from home, and he was nervous at first. He was scared that what some people saw as talent might be nothing more than a gust of wind, that he'd fail and be sent home. He was nineteen, still very insecure and edgy.

As it turned out, he needn't have worried. Half the people there for the summer felt exactly the same way. Keanu liked the other kids—and America. Even in rural Pennsylvania, there was a looseness, an easiness of spirit that was missing in Toronto. The group only staged one production, a version of Shakespeare's *Romeo and Juliet*, but there was still plenty to take in. Keanu absorbed it all before starting the Volvo and heading north again.

Toronto seemed small and constricting after a summer away. But Keanu eagerly returned to Leah Posluns. He'd learned enough to know how much he still had to learn. So he dove into his studies, ready to make the most of his time there.

The students were encouraged to attend as many auditions as possible. Not only did that help prepare them for the future, when auditions would be a regular part of their lives, but it also offered an opportunity for them to practice all they'd been learning in school.

Keanu was no different from the others. He tried out for anything and everything, which was how he ended up being cast in two films. Neither *Prodigal* nor *Flying* made any impact outside Canada— or that much of an impact in the country, for that matter—but they had a huge effect on Keanu. Film work was great. Exacting perhaps, with its short, endless retakes, but fun. Most of the time he was just sitting around, watching and learning. Best of all, it paid well. A few days on the set brought home the same as a month on the stage. While it wasn't necessarily more satisfying—and he hated the early morning calls—it offered things that appealed to him. Movies were like records, in a way. You bought albums by bands you liked; you saw movies by actors you admired.

This, he decided, might be the way to go.

But first came more pressing concerns. He was now in his senior year at Leah Posluns, and the graduating class always put on a production. This time it would be *Romeo and Juliet*. Keanu was cast as Mercutio. Not the starring role, but one which offered less romance and more substance.

Playing the part was almost as great a turning point as discovering the love for acting inside himself. It had depth, exuberance and tragedy—everything he could desire in a character. It caught something in him; even today, he considers it the best role ever written.

"There was something essential about himself that he needed to express through Mercutio," was director Lewis Baumander's evaluation. Baumander was a senior teacher at the school and in charge of the year's production. "There's a profound sadness ultimately to that character that manifests itself in a kind of manic energy. And Keanu had access to so many kinds of primal kinds of impulses and feelings."

It went over well, and he, of course, was an excellent Mercutio, outshining the Romeo. And when it was done, so were his schooldays. Now Keanu had to go out and face the real world.

He already had his plans made. He knew what his skills were, how best to use them, and where to do it. He was going to move to California and become a film actor. Movies were real work, but thousands of people all over the world saw the results. And Los Angeles was the place where they made them.

It could have remained little more than a dream if it hadn't been for former Leah Posluns student Steven Stern, who was now directing television movies in Hollywood. Keanu had auditioned for him in Toronto for a small role in a Disney production, and Stern had been impressed.

"I told him to take the script home and read for the lead," he recalled. Stern was serious enough, over the protests of studio executives, to fly Keanu out for a screen test. He got the part, and knew he had to be westward bound.

Paul Aaron was glad to do whatever he could to help and offered his house as a place to stay. He'd encouraged Keanu's career so far, and seen him succeed well beyond the dreams of most student actors. Keanu had already put together a strong resume, a powerful mix of stage, television and film appearances. Aaron had the experience, and the contacts, to give him a good start in Hollywood. It was a business where talent wasn't enough at the beginning. It was also who you knew, and who you could get in to see. Every advantage would be useful.

He still loved the theater, but its opportunities, particularly in a city like Toronto, were very limited. He could go to New York, but there the odds would be stacked against him. And there was only a limited amount of work available. No, if he was leaving, it would be for somewhere warm. He felt he had a shot in Hollywood. He photographed well, the cinematographers told him. It was one of the most important qualities for film work, they said.

He sat down and talked to Patricia. She supported his decision. Acting was the first thing he'd ever taken completely seriously. If he was going to leave and try his luck, when he was young and free was the best time.

Even before he'd left his home, Aaron had set him up to be represented by Erwin Stoff, who was then just starting his management company. By the time Keanu arrived on the West coast, his photograph and resume would have been circulated to casting directors.

Keanu packed up his clothes, his records, and his stereo, filling up the Volvo until only the driver's seat was empty. Now he felt a pang of sadness about leaving his mother and his sisters. But at the same time there was a huge sense of excitement. This was the road trip of a lifetime!

It was 1986. Keanu was twenty. He said goodbye, started the car, and left Toronto in the rearview mirror. A new life was calling.

CHAPTER TWO

There were two routes Keanu could take to Los Angeles—he could drive the the Trans-Canadian Highway to Vancouver and then go down the Pacific coast, or he could journey across America. Keanu decided on America. After sixteen years north of the border, he needed a change. And, if he was going to live in the U.S. and play Americans on film, getting a good look at the country and its people could only help.

Surprisignly, the Volvo held up well. Old, decrepit, and loaded down with gear, it still managed to complete the trip without any major breakdowns. It seemed like a good omen. With no car trouble and work very likely waiting, Keanu was feeling good and lucky as he finally reached L.A.

The first thing he did was check in with Aaron's talent management agency, Elsboy Entertainment, which was set to start representing him. The news he received wasn't anything he really wanted to hear.

"I was informed [they] were having trouble getting me in to see some casting agents because of my name. It had an ethnicity to it that they found was getting in the way. And so they said that I had to change my name. And that freaked me out completely."

In staid Toronto the name Keanu had given him no problem. And it hadn't troubled Disney. But elsewhere in Hollywood, where things were supposed to be laid-back, free and easy, where anything went, he was having probelms because of a Hawaiian name. Hawaii was part of the United States. It didn't make sense. For a moment he was tempted not to bother unpacking, but jump straight back in the car and head north again. At least there you got a chance.

But his manager calmed him down. It was just for a while, until he was known. As soon as that happened, he could be Keanu again. In the meantime, though, they needed to come up with something good, something appealing.

So, on his first night in America's city of dreams,

Keanu sat on his motel bed and came up with a list of alternate names for himself. Some were grand, like Page Templeton III. Others were ridiculously outlandish, like Chuck Spidina.

The one everyone agreed on was K.C. Reeves.

"That was a terrible, terrible phase," he recalled, "which lasted about a month." He hated doing it; it wasn't him. "When I went to auditions, I'd tell them my name was Keanu anyway."

Stoff rapidly proved his worth as a manager by landing Keanu an agent. And not just any agent, but Hildy Gottlieb Hill, who was head of talent at ICM. Keanu soon won her over.

"In 20 minutes I was crazy about him," she said, and signed him before she even knew he could act. Before he could turn around, she was sending him out on more auditions for television movies. Keanu still looked very young and vulnerable, with long, dark hair hanging straight down over his face and a body that hadn't fully developed yet. His style wasn't that of a California hunk, but he'd be ideal for adolescent parts. The turnaround was fast, the roles looked good on the resume, and his face would be seen by millions of people—ideal exposure. And more than that, they'd help him get his Screen Actors Guild card—the passport to better roles and better pay.

Despite his impressive credentials, the directors Keanu encountered seemed surprised that a Canadian could really act. Or that, with his unique manner, Keanu could quickly get to the heart of a character. In fact, one of them commented that he had "more acting tics than a cheap watch."

But it didn't seem to matter. Very soon he was beginning to land parts. *Letting Go*, the Disney production, helped pay the rent during the rest of 1985, and was quickly followed by *Act of Vengeance*, a good Charles Bronson drama about fighting corruption in the coal unions. Then came *Babes in Toyland*—not a remake of the Victor Herbert operetta that Disney had popularized, but a disappointing fairytale that starred a young Drew Barrymore alongside veterans like Richard Mulligan, Eileen Brennan, and Noriyuki "Pat" Morita. Keanu didn't have much to do in any of them, a few lines at best, nothing more. But he'd started, he'd broken the barrier. He was in the movies.

Off the set he might have looked a bit of a wreck, with hair all over the place and old, torn clothes, riding around on the motorcycle he'd bought after the Volvo finally died. But at the soundstage or on location he was perfectly professional, all business.

Under The Influence cracked the Screen Actors Guild requirements. It was also the first production where he'd had to report to work very early.

"I thought this was . . . unfair. It's hard to act in the morning. The muse isn't even awake."

But the muse evidently struggled well enough in her sleep to get Keanu noticed. As soon as he was finished there, he was working on yet another TV movie, *Brotherhood of Justice*, a message film about good kids trying to reclaim their high school from vandals. Then he was up for a bigger film role.

Again, it wasn't much; if you blinked a few times you'd have missed him. And there was an irony that Keanu had traveled almost 4,000 miles from Toronto to make his feature film debut in a movie about ice hockey. Sometimes, during the filming, he even wondered if he'd been hired simply because he could play the game. But on the rink he knew what he was doing, which was more than could be said for a lot of the others, some of whom could barely skate, let alone play the game.

By rights, *Youngblood* should have done well, if not spectacularly. Hockey was an active, violent sport, the type to get the blood pumping. *Slapshot* hadn't been a disaster. And this one had Rob Lowe as its star. He was still a big draw then, before his fall from grace. Rob Lowe and action sounded like guaranteed box office money. But it was an instance of the public staying away in droves. What

should have been Keanu's big, bursting moment—
his entrance into Hollwood films—proved to be
more like a damp firecracker.

For all that, he wasn't discouraged. He'd done
his work, and what little of it there was had been
fine. When all was said and done, he *had* been in a
movie. It simply reaffirmed everything he'd felt
while making the two features in Canada—this
was the way to go. Movies could accommodate
someone like him, who knew the principles of acting but had his own, unique style.

His natural tendency was towards the active:
moving, walking around, talking to himself, laugh-
ing unexpectedly. It took people by surprise. But
that was just the way he was. Put him in front of
a camera and that all went away; he could be a
stone if it was necessary. Then, out in the sunlight
again, it was back to the manic.

Part of his earnings from *Youngblood* went towards a bass guitar and amplifier. Music had been
such a big part of his life for so long, and it had
intrigued him so much that he finally decided it
was time to learn to play for himself. And the bass,
with only four strings and no chords to learn,
looked like the easiest instrument to tackle.

He knew that it would take time to master, but
that didn't stop him from thrashing away, figuring

out the bass lines to Ramones' songs and letting the music pump. In its own way, music had the same freedom as riding a bike. You could go fast, you were on your own, and the world seemed far away.

The world wouldn't stay away from Keanu, though. *Youngblood* might have flopped disastrously, and that was depressing for his first cinematic outing, but the wispy memories would soon be erased by *River's Edge*.

In a time when films about teenagers automatically brought to mind the work of John Hughes (*The Breakfast Club*, etc.), *River's Edge* was very disturbingly real. Based, albeit fairly peripherally, on an incident that had happened in 1981 in Milpitas, in northern California, the movie was as much social comment and morality play as it was a story.

In the tale the film told, John (Daniel Roebuck) had strangled his girlfriend for no obvious reason and left her naked body by the river. At school, questioned by his friends as to where the girl, Jamie, was, he flatly told them what had happened. They didn't believe him. Only when they saw the body for themselves was there any realization in their eyes.

From there Layne (Crispin Glover), the speed freak "leader" of the group, took charge. John had to be protected, even though he didn't seem to care. The body needed to be disposed of, and John sent out of town. With his best friend Matt (Keanu) along, he made the rounds of friends, trying to get money to help his cause.

But Matt, who had troubles enough of his own at home—a sociopathic younger brother who tormented their sister, a mother more caught up in her idiotic live-in lover than in her children—had already told the police about the murder. Even if he couldn't put his feelings into words, at least he had some pity for the dead girl.

Layne left John with Feck (Dennis Hopper), the only adult he trusted, a former biker who was now a warped recluse and lived with an inflatable doll. He, too, had murdered his girlfriend, or so he claimed. But he had killed her because he loved her. Feck was the only person, other than a teacher, who showed any passion about anything in the film.

Over the course of a night, things changed completely. Layne's group didn't fall into line behind him. Even his girlfriend, Clarissa, played by Ione Skye, ended up with Matt. And Feck shot John.

At Jamie's funeral, a gruesome open casket affair, the teens passed the coffin, then sat down. Again, no emotion was shown. It had happened, it was over.

River's Edge caught the reviewers' attention not just because it was very good, but for what it said about American families and American youth. And what it was saying were things that people didn't want to hear. The kids weren't just alienated; most of them had given up altogether, and existed in a world that consisted solely of themselves and a few friends. They had emotions, but they were so well-hidden that they might as well not have existed. Getting stoned and getting drunk were their activities. And why should it have been any different? Their parents didn't seem to care about their comings and goings. The world was a shell, and it was empty inside.

Only Matt, who had the courage to risk vilification from his friends by telling the police about Jamie's murder and then turning his back on Layne, seemed to have a fighting chance of becoming a fully formed adult. He was the only one who seemed to care—however vaguely—about *anything* at all.

This was what music had been saying for a decade: that there was no future, that the emotional landscape was barren and bleak, like the aftermath of a nuclear war.

It was powerful stuff. These weren't even bad kids; they came from decent homes, some from money. Something had gone radically wrong. Thankfully, there was no finger-pointing, no implicit moral in the last five minutes. It worked on the emotions by its deadness, not its life.

The critics agreed that it was an excellent film. As David Ansen summed up in *Newsweek*, "Some may gag on this daring, disturbing movie; few will be able to shake it off." In *New York*, David Denby called it ". . . the most disturbing movie I have seen in the nearly nine years I have held this job . . . another triumph for the independent film movement . . . this is the only one that matters." That sentiment was echoed by *People*, "*River's Edge* may often be crude and disorganized, but here at last is a different kind of youth picture: one that matters." *People* added that it was, "the best and boldest American movie so far this year . . ."

Like it or hate it, the film was impossible to ignore. The debates it provoked about the way American youth and American families were heading overshadowed the picture itself, as well as its performances. Only Layne was really singled out for comment, due to his stylized, affected, and often androgynous manner, and even then it was with a sense of revulsion. But he was the one who stood out, if only because he was the only character with any kind of flamboyance, however skewed.

As Matt, Keanu gave a bravura reading of a mixed-up adolescent, "a decent boy struggling for clarity," as *New York* voiced it. *Time* praised him for the "exemplary restraint" in his acting, and *People* mentioned how Matt was "sharply characterized." And he showed that under the leather jacket and behind the vacant, stoned grin, there was a good kid who sometimes peeked out. It was a difficult role to fill without seeming maudlin or goody two-shoes, a very fine line. But Keanu walked it perfectly.

Of course, his own adolescence wasn't too far behind him, and was certainly still close enough for him to recapture the confused emotions of being seventeen. As the foil to Crispin Glover's Layne, he was the sensible one who came closest to facing reality and building a bridge between the alienated state of the teenagers and the real world.

But even Matt didn't know what he was feeling a lot of the time. Keanu was able to give him the innocence and vulnerability that he himself possessed, which would remain with him for several years.

To be involved in such a prestigious movie at this early stage in his career—particularly after the flop of *Youngblood*—was a great boost to his confidence. It had seemed that he might have to return to television work to keep his name known. Now, though, there was no need for that. Even if it wasn't a box office success, *River's Edge* was widely reviewed and seen by people in the industry.

It was his breakthrough, although at the time he just seemed like part of the ensemble. The film truly highlighted his best qualities. Not only could he act very well, but he was also very handsome in an unconventional, youthful way. The name Keanu Reeves began to mean a little something in Los Angeles.

And Los Angeles was beginning to mean something to him. Arriving, quite literally, as an alien, he'd quickly adapted to the native customs. His speech was soon peppered with words like "cool," "gnarly," or "weird." He tooled around town on his motorcycle, often late at night, enjoying the sensation of speed—and often receiving tickets for his pleasure. He felt at home in L.A.; he had a free and easy lifestyle that seemed perfect. He had his work to focus his mind, and when he had time to himself, there were plenty of distractions.

He'd even begun to read, as if to make up for

the schoolwork that had never come easily. He devoured everything; Russian writers, modern physics, they were all grist to the mill. It was as if California had brought him completely to life. Part of it was living alone. He loved his mother, and she'd been very helpful and supportive of him. But in being by himself, in depending purely on himself, he'd been able to grow and mature. He hadn't completely found himself yet, but he was much closer than he'd ever been in Toronto.

He was also making money doing exactly the thing he wanted. Following *River's Edge* there was no shortage of offers for his acting skills. They were all teenage roles, but that was almost to be expected. Keanu still looked young. He even walked like a teenager.

So it was no big surprise that for his next role he played another seventeen-year-old boy.

Permanent Record was the flip side of *River's Edge*, in a way, a shift from teen murder to teen suicide. For the first time Keanu was the movie's star—not too shabby for what was only his third picture.

He played Chris Townsend, the best friend of high-achieving student David Sinclair (Alan Boyce). The two attended a performing arts school in a fictional city (actually a curious mixture of Portland and Newport, Oregon). The two played in the same band and were involved in the same extracurricular activities. Chris thought he knew everything about his buddy. But he had no idea of the pressure David felt.

On the night Chris had a party, David wandered away in search of fresh air, as he told one of the girls there. He walked down the road from the house to a cliff and gazed out over the water. Unbeknownst to David, Chris had followed, and was hiding, intending to surprise him.

However, when Chris popped out, David was no longer there.

It was presumed to be an accident. Only later, when Chris received a letter from David, a suicide note mailed before his death, did he realize the truth. And the truth was difficult to deal with, for Chris and all of David's other friends.

For, obviously, nobody had really known or understood him—not his parents, not the girl he slept with. And coming to terms with that, as much as the fact of the suicide itself, was hard. With the principal's blessing they arranged a memorial service for the school. When it was quashed by the superintendent, Chris finally lost his temper, broke a window, and was expelled.

But in the end, there was a resolution of a sort. Chris was reinstated. His band recorded a song for which David had written the melody and Chris the lyrics. And in the middle of a school performance of Gilbert and Sullivan's *H.M.S. Pinafore*, one of the girls sang it.

It wasn't understanding, it could never be that, but it was acceptance, and farewell.

Permanent Record had the chance to be as powerful as *River's Edge*. It dealt with a touchy subject, one that has occurred to most teenagers at one point or another. And, for its first half, it looked as if it might really be powerful—well-directed, beautifully photographed, and with a script that avoided the usual platitudes and cliches—which made it even more of a shame when, towards the end, it crumbled into television movie territory. The close was simply too pat, too rounded, and too melodramatic. It was sad to watch all the possibilities fade away to nothing, or, as *Newsweek* wrote, "Instead of learning about the real inner resources of kids coping with grief, we learn once again about the evasive strategies of Hollywood melodrama."

Certainly the cast held no blame. They all did fine work. Keanu, as the emotional center of the film, had a great deal of weight to carry, and proved himself to be "a remarkably honest, natural actor, [who] doesn't make a false move." He had to run the gamut of emotions, from joy to numbness to anger to sorrrow, and pulled them all off perfectly.

While much of that could be attributed to his training as an actor, that kind of craftsmanship can only take a person so far. Beyond that lies art, for that's what his performance became. His portrayal of a teenager, cocky at times, completely unsure of himself at others, was utterly on the money. Keanu even performed most of his character's onscreen guitar work himself. Chris was quite different from Matt in *River's Edge*. He could—and did—feel quite deeply, and if he wasn't able to fully articulate everything running around inside, he was still able to let it out, through rage or tears or music.

In spite of a few wild ways, especially his driving, Chris was a good kid. All of them in the film were. The beer drinking and pot smoking were part of teenage ritual, rather than symptoms of anything wrong. They were attempting to make sense of the world, not cut themselves off from it. They were all involved with things outside themselves.

More than anything in the wake of *River's Edge*, *Permanent Record* established Keanu as an actor to watch closely. It was obvious that he was a genuine talent, someone who stood out from the pack. He *was* Chris while he was onscreen; the viewer never doubted that. Even the character's guitar playing was his own, the result of several years of practice on the instrument.

The danger seemed that he could become stereotyped as the troubled teen, a darker version of Molly Ringwald, which might lead to the kind of path that would prove a dead end. In the long run that would do him no justice, nor his career any favors.

But there didn't seem to be any way out of it. He simply looked too young to play adults. For the moment he wasn't too worried. After all, he was still only twenty-three. There was plenty of time left to think about the future.

Permanent Record didn't do much business at the box office. Most reviewers didn't even bother with it, although it dealt with a delicate and topical subject. Not very heavily promoted, it didn't last long in the theaters before vanishing and then appearing on video. And, given its ending, a small screen seemed a better format for it.

Keanu, though, had already moved on to other projects. The others in the cast of *Permanent Record* would appear here and there, mostly on television. But he had his priorities right. He'd graduated and escaped from that medium. He'd been given his chances, and now he was out to make the most of them.

What he knew, even if producers and casting agents didn't yet, was that he had a fine gift for comedy as well as drama. The timing of it came naturally to him, and he certainly didn't mind making himself look foolish to generate a laugh. So when the opportunity to show that side of his skill came along, he jumped at it.

The Night Before held another major attraction for Keanu. By now he was a confirmed motorcycle addict; it was his only mode of transportation. In the film he got to ride a Moto Guzzi, a beautiful Italian machine, around Los Angeles at "130 miles per hour . . . I called the bike Guzzi Moto, like Quasimodo. It was a heavy bike."

But Keanu being funny and riding a motorcycle wasn't likely to bring audiences out, not at this stage in his career. That was a shame, because it offered some genuinely funny moments. The tale of one of the most disastrous prom nights in history, it starred Keanu as a young man who awoke in an alley to find his date and his wallet—not to mention the sports car he'd borrowed from his father—mysteriously vanished. His attempts to find them took increasingly surreal turns as the story progressed, and that proved to be the film's problem. Not a teen vehicle, nor a bizarre adult comedy, it was lost, and left the theaters as quickly—and as quietly—as it arrived.

From there Keanu headed east, back to Pennsylvania, a place he hadn't seen since his summer with the Hedgerow Theater. This was for *The Price of Pennsylvania,* filmed outside Pittsburgh. As soon as he arrived, Keanu rented a Harley-Davidson for the duration of shooting. Very soon he was thrilling himself and other members of the cast and crew who went with him.

"I used to like to ride through the woods," he said, ". . . at night with the lights off, with maybe two other people on the back, and we'd tell each other what we saw. It was very cool."

He enjoyed the filming as much as the riding, portraying a young man obsessed with death who lived in a decaying Pennsylvania mining town. It even featured the loss of Keanu's onscreen virginity, and as Amy Madigan's boyfriend, he had to undergo the traditional apologies during the filming of their sex scene together,

"You have to say . . . 'Excuse me if I get excited,' and 'I'm sorry if I don't,' you know?"

It was the type of thing that has plagued actors for as long as there have been sex scenes in movies.

As it was, for all the work by director Ron Nyswaner, Keanu, and the rest of the cast, *The Price of Pennsylvania* never even saw a theatrical release, although Keanu insisted it was a good film. Instead it went directly to video, where its shelf life in the stores proved quite short.

After one small hit, and three flops, Keanu really needed something big to put his career back on track. Not that he was bothered much, as long as the work was interesting, varied and challenging to him as an actor. But, despite his talent, with those statistics, he was in danger of falling back into the great pit of young actors who might have been great but ended up lost.

So he auditioned for a role in the upcoming *Dangerous Liaisons*. The stars had already been set— Glenn Close, John Malkovich, and Swoosie Kurtz— and the picture would be directed by Stephen Frears, who'd made his name in Britain with *My Beautiful Laundrette* and *Prick Up Your Ears*. It would be a big, bold production, an adaptation of Choderlos de Laclos' scandalous eighteenth-century French novel *Les Liaisons Dangereuses*, which Christopher Hampton had made into a successful stage play. And while the character Keanu hoped to play was young, this was hardly the type of teen vehicle he been involved with before.

But, as it was, he almost didn't make it as far as the movie . . .

CHAPTER THREE

Keanu had endured wrecks on his motorcycle before. He already had a scar on his calf from one accident, and another on his left knee from being hit by a car at the corner of Hollywood and Normandie in Los Angeles. That pile up landed him in the hospital and totaled his bike, and he just managed to avoid more serious injury by leaping off the machine before impact.

Those two accidents had been bad enough. Many people would have taken them as warnings and bought a car. Not Keanu, though; he loved the freedom of a motorcycle, and, above all, the opportunity for speed that it offered. So perhaps it was inevitable that there'd be more problems.

This time, though, it went beyond mere problem.

While up for the role of the Chevalier de Darceny in *Dangerous Liaisons*, he was out riding, passing some free time, and, as he put it, "I ran into a mountain."

And the mountain proved remarkably unforgiving. Keanu ended up in the hospital flat on his back, where he found out that he had gotten the part in the movie, and also that he'd be carrying around a long, nasty scar on his stomach for the rest of his life.

Even that didn't discourage him from motorcycles. He simply loved them; they'd become the great passion of his life. Outside of acting and music, they were probably the only passion of his life. Once he'd been discharged from hospital, Keanu went out and bought another bike, a vintage 1972 Norton 850 Commando, a true British classic. If it scared him to get on and ride, he didn't show it. This *was* being alive, riding around, looking and seeing.

As soon as he'd fully recuperated, he was off to work on the movie. *Dangerous Liaisons* was a tale of mental cruelty and seduction, detatched for the most part, and viewed like a game of chess. Hampton wrote the script, basing it on his play, and the words flowed and parried with rare intelligence for a Hollywood film.

But really, the only American things in this movie were the accents of the leading actors. The rest—the settings, the wit, the decadence—were decidedly European. As Frears's U.S. debut, it was daring, the kind of film that seemed destined, by its attitude, to find only a marginal audience in this country.

But Frears certainly made the most of it, making the reported $14 million budget look much more expansive with gorgeous photography of beautiful chateaux.

Still, this was a film that was mostly driven by its dialogue, and there was no shortage of that. As the Marquise de Merteuil and the Vicomte de Valmont, Glenn Close and John Malkovich sparred with and challenged each other. Former lovers and close friends, they shared a deliciously amoral view of the world, seducing not for romance, but for revenge and reputation.

Keanu played Darceny, a penniless young nobleman who became a pawn in their games. A sensitive music lover, he was introdcued to the virginal Cecile and became her music teacher, quickly falling in love with her.

The Marquise informed Cecile's mother of the innocent, unconsummated romance, and suggested she remove her daughter to the country—conveniently, to the house where Valmont was a guest.

Valmont, of course, seduced her, and could have had Madame de Tourval also—but held back, feeling tenderness for her.

He confessed his feelings to the Marquise, never realizing that she had long been in love with him. Playing the game like a chess match, she took a new lover—Darceny, although for the present she chose to keep the fact secret.

It became open knowledge when Valmont's servant spotted them together. By then Valmont was involved with Madame de Tourval. At the urging of the Marquise, he broke with her, to claim his reward. But he never received it.

For the Marquise had informed Darceny that Cecile, the girl he loved, had become just another of Valmont's conquests.

Darceny challenged Valmont to a duel, and killed him. But not before they had a few last words. There was a message to Madame de Tourval containing his true feelings, which let her die in peace. And there was a packet of letters, the ones the Marquise had sent him detailing their plots and games, to be circulated around Paris.

The Marquise lived, but she might as well not

have. She was a social outcast, booed at the Opera, and condemned to a solitary life.

It was heady stuff, a film full of twists and turns where language was the most important tool—quite a rarity for Hollywood. Although it was a major theatrical release, and there was hope of it attracting a mass audience through the drawing power of its stars, it never had a huge chance of box office success. It was simply too intellectual.

Not that that stopped the critics, or the Academy, from rhapsodizing over it. *Dangerous Liaisons* was nominated for seven Academy Awards, including Best Picture, and ended up with three.

In *Newsweek*, David Ansen called the film "as steamy as dry ice . . . nasty, decadent fun," and commented that, "It says something about Frears's vision that he can cast actors as seemingly disparate as Keanu Reeves, Mildred Natwick and Swoosie Kurtz and mold them into a perfectly plausible 18th century ensemble," while *People* said that "[Frears] . . . makes characters of 200 years ago seem as near as next door . . . a seductive, scary, savagely witty look at the unchanging way of the world," adding, ". . . don't expect *Masterpiece Theatre* gentility. This baby bites."

And that was a very true comment. There were

plenty of sharp teeth and barbs in the lines. It was a chess game, with Cecile, Madame de Tourval, and Darceny as the pawns directed by the Marquise and Valmont. None of them came away unbruised or with innocence intact.

The movie showcased John Malkovich and Glenn Close in the leading roles. Both had already proven themselves to be among the country's leading actors. Together they sizzled, the pitch of malevolence rising with each meeting between them. It showed what Hollywood was capable of, but very rarely achieved—drama and intensity as strong as the theater—and written with intelligence.

That was why Keanu had been so eager to be involved with the project. He was, after all, a well-trained actor with strong roots in theater. Being chosen as Darceny meant acceptance of him as someone who could go well beyond the modern teenage stereotype he was becoming known for.

His part was small, but pivotal to the plot. He had to show the great naivete of the young, and mix it with overwhelming surges of emotion. Indeed, his first scene, at the Opera, had him crying, moved to tears by the beauty of the music. Not that it was easy to film. Tears didn't come readily to

Keanu in real life, although, as an artist he "kind of like[d] to suffer."

As it was, his tears took six hours to fall.

"Stephen Frears came up to me," he recalled, "and said, 'Can't you think of your mother being *dead* or something? You're a method actor. Isn't there *something* you can do?'"

Eventually there was, but it was the greatest difficulty he'd encountered so far in his career, and the biggest challenge of the movie. Overall, the filming was a wonderful experience, especially being accepted as an equal by such talents as Malkovich, whom Keanu described as "the heaviest fuckin' actor, man—he's great." In his turn, having seen Keanu at work and at play, Malkovich was able to make this assessment of Keanu:

"He's the archetypal troubled young American. He's like your younger brother, someone you should be helping out in some way. He doesn't invite it. I don't think he would like it much. But if you're older, you feel you should protect him."

It was a reasonable view. Keanu was—and to a large extent would remain—a mass of confusion and contradictions. There was a certainty in his acting. But beyond that, he projected a vulnerability that seemed unusual for a twenty-three year old, mixed with a desire to go through life so quickly that was positively dangerous. So it was hardly strange that Malkovich, a generation older and wiser, should have felt the protective urge.

But really, Keanu didn't need it. He was well aware of his own tendencies—his scattershot, haphazard approach to life—and he understood that was just the way he was. All that really mattered was the acting. That was the center of everything. The rest was, well, just life. Given work on a good film and his motorcycle, Keanu was happy.

And *Dangerous Liaisons* proved to be a very good film. As a career move, it was a very good one for Keanu, pushing him into a new area and showing a different side of his abilities. His appearance in something so prestigious, particularly after two flops, forced people to look at him more seriously and realize that he was a person whose talent wouldn't evaporate as soon as he looked old enough to play adults.

He had wanted to prove that he was vital, and he'd done it. Hollywood would hardly be at his feet because of it, but it would mean more offers, and more work. Above all, more *interesting* work.

CHAPTER FOUR

1989 brought Keanu the role that would both make him and become a millstone around his neck, his personal Frankenstein. As Ted "Theodore" Logan in *Bill and Ted's Excellent Adventure* he'd truly break through to public consciousness. Unfortunately he'd also be so identified with the character that for several years, until *Speed*, really, plenty of people would just assume that Keanu *was* Ted.

In itself that might not have been so bad, except for the fact that Ted was a complete airhead. His speech consisted of short sentences, all peppered with "dude" and "excellent," which, to be fair, had their place in Keanu's vocabulary. So, naturally, the assumption was that Keanu wasn't too bright either, when nothing could be further from the truth. He might not have finished high school, but he'd continued to educate himself, reading everything from Dostoevski to Thomas Mann to Stephen Hawking—a wide and accomplished range.

It seemed strange that such a relatively minor film could color public perception of him so much. And it hindered any plans he had of being taken seriously as an actor for a few years. Not until *Point Break*, and, especially, *My Own Private Idaho*, would he be able to break out of the confines he'd created.

Certainly no one imagined that *Bill and Ted's Excellent Adventure* would have the impact it did. Released with very little fanfare, barely reviewed—and disliked by those who did write about it—the movie seemed condemned to a very short life in the theaters before being resurrected on video. But something odd happened. A few people, mostly young people, saw it and liked it. There was something in it, the over the top presentation, the innate joy of the characters being smarter (and luckier) than they looked and outwitting the adults, that teens could relate to. They told other kids. Soon the movie was doing well. Very well indeed; against all the odds it would go on to become one of the top-grossing pictures of the year.

Bill and Ted had a heavy metal band, Wyld Stallyns. The fact that neither of them could play and there weren't any other members were minor obstacles. They were going to be huge someday.

For the moment, though, they were both in school, and failing history. Their last chance at passing would come with the orals—and they'd both need grades of A+ to graduate. For Ted, failure meant that his father, a police detective, would send him to military school—in Alaska.

With less than twenty-four hours before the exam, it looked hopeless. Neither was good at bookwork. But help came in the form of a phone booth tumbling from the sky, disgorging a man called Rufus (George Carlin), who'd been sent to help them.

For, it seemed, the music of Wyld Stallyns would be important to the future, bringing peace and enlightenment, and giving Bill and Ted almost godlike status.

First, though, they had to pass history. With the phone booth, which was a time machine, the push buttons and a directory, they could take a little trip. . . .

The original idea had been to collect a couple of historical figures to speak at the oral exam. But it all got wildly out of hand. Which was how Abe Lincoln, Napoleon, Billy the Kid, Socrates, Genghis

Khan, and Beethoven all ended up crammed in a phone booth, traveling through the centuries to San Dimas, California.

Rounding them up was only half the battle. Once they were loose in the late twentieth century, chaos ensued, and jail—although, thanks to a little time machine trickery, freeing them proved easy.

With barely any time to spare, the extremely motley crew reached the high school auditorium. Of course, the presentation proved to be a work of genius, each historical figure doing exactly what he or she did best, all coordinated by Bill and Ted. It wasn't a history final—it was a rock concert, complete with lights and a huge array of keyboards for Beethoven to demonstrate his skills on in manic fashion. And, when it was done, the kids in the audience reacted as they would at any show—flicking their lighters for an encore.

Needless to say, Bill and Ted both passed with flying colors. They'd graduated, and the specter of military school had vanished. And, more importantly, they were now free to return to the fifteenth century and liberate the two princesses—the "babes"—they'd encountered on their travels. But, best of all, the legend of Wyld Stallyns lived on, and would soon flourish.

* * *

The movie was ridiculous, impossible, and great fun. For every high school kid, giving an oral presentation like Bill and Ted's was one of those hilarious fantasies, a way of pushing the teacher's face in the mud. The film ridiculed Americans' knowledge of world history, taught them something, and laughed out loud while it was doing it. There was a lot more going on in it than the critics were willing to admit, an intelligence running through the script that they seemed to miss.

People, one of the few magazines that even bothered to review the film, dismissed it as "a tribute to ignorance and a monument to dweebs everywhere," calling the script "feeble" and assessing the work of Keanu and Alex Winter, who played Bill, as coming "from the Chevy Chase-Sean Penn School of Charmlessness."

It was an unnecessarily harsh look at a film that was meant as pure entertainment, in its own way portraying the late 1980s with the same kind of affection *American Graffiti* had shown for the 1950s. Bill and Ted were dumb, but in a sweet way that had more to do with Laurel and Hardy than Chase or Penn.

And to make the characters come across that way took a great deal of skill. Keanu and Winter were the center of the film, onscreen for almost every scene, never an easy task.

Keanu, in particular, had a very lovable quality as Ted. As usual, his hair stopped just short of being long, but was still shaggy, and he had the awkward, loping walk of a teenager still not comfortable with his full height. He fit into the role so perfectly it could have been written for him; he *was* Ted.

While that would create problems in the future, for now it helped the film become a surprising success. Teenagers could relate to Bill and Ted. Rather than treating them as idiots or failures, the movie slyly celebrated them. You still laughed at them, but you also laughed with them.

Without any doubt, this bit of light relief was the turning point in Keanu's career. After the meaty, dramatic roles he'd enjoyed in *River's Edge*, *Permanent Record*, and *Dangerous Liaisons*, there was a definite irony in that. But Keanu had always been a rounded performer, with as much flair for comedy as drama. He had the perfect light touch for this type of part, with wonderful timing, letting the laughs come easily, rather than clumsily building to the punch lines. His Ted was gentle, bumbling, and fairly inarticulate, and we loved him. In a way, he was the other side of Darceny from *Dangerous*

Liaisons, equally naive about the real world, but skipping free of its evil. This wasn't the first comedy Keanu had been involved in by any means, but it was the first that more than a handful of people saw, and certainly the first to be widely talked about.

And Keanu himself seemed to show his gentle, reserved side in public. He, too, tended towards the inarticulate in interviews, uncomfortable when he had to talk about himself.

"Ted," he admitted later, after a few years of being stereotyped by the role, "hung a label on me, and I hung it on myself, to a certain extent."

Not that he was too bothered then as to what people thought of him. He was happy, and that was what counted. Like everyone else connected with *Bill and Ted's Excellent Adventure*, he was astonished that it became as popular as it did—a movie with no known stars. Indeed, there was only one recognizable name in the entire cast—George Carlin.

But the movie did succeed, leaving critics to shake their heads over the way America seemed to be gravitating towards the stupid.

There was no denying, however, that Keanu showed a real presence in the film. He seemed to fill the screen whenever he was on camera. That was much more evident here than in his previous work, which had demanded other things from him. What was definitely apparent was the way he'd grown as an actor. In *River's Edge,* his performance had been powerful but still tentative. Much the same applied to Chris in *Permanent Record;* he was still being formed as an actor, still learning.

As Ted, the best thing to do was let himself go, have fun with the character, and he did. He reveled in the role, and it showed. Keanu had found something deep inside himself, and let it run free.

It was great acting, far better than the critics ever gave him credit for. But after his other roles, it sealed his fate for a while. In all his roles, he'd played teenagers, and this one further established his reputation as one of cinema's troubled youth. Breaking out of that mold would be difficult, indeed, impossible, for a while. And when he tried, people wouldn't be too keen on accepting a different Keanu from the goofball they'd come to recognize.

The teenagers of the 1980s would become the slacker generation, Generation X, whatever label could be found, of the 1990s. And they could accept Keanu for what he was—essentially one of them, growing, expanding his horizons, and trying to define himself, however unsuccessfully.

"He's a hero for the slacker generation," said Keith Mayerson, a student in Stephen Prina's course on Keanu Revves at the Art Center College of Design in Pasadena. "He's a little vacant, a little inarticulate, but he's still beautiful and he still gets the girl."

That was an accurate way of looking at Keanu. He was handsome in an unusual way, one that intrigued rather than overwhelmed. He was vacant and inarticulate to a point, as were many of his generation, but his lack of words hinted at hidden depths rather than any lack of intelligence. And, as in most of his movies, he *had* ended up with the girl.

Given the success of *Bill and Ted's Excellent Adventure* and Keanu's obvious flair for comedy, it was no surprise that he was flooded with scripts offering him offbeat, humorous teenage roles. The opportunity was there to star in any number of knockoff "Bill and Ted" movies.

That wouldn't have offered him any challenge, though. And if the role didn't stretch him as an actor, Keanu wasn't interested in the film. It didn't matter whether it was an independent production or from a major studio, it was the quality he was interested in. The fast buck could always be made, but that wasn't acting, it was simply reciting lines.

And he hadn't gone into the business to do that.

He couldn't resist the offer to join the cast of Ron Howard's new movie, *Parenthood*. Keanu would only have a small role, but, while he'd still be playing someone younger than himself, it would show him in a completely different light.

Howard, of course, was no stranger to moviemaking, having had a huge success with *Splash* after a fairly long acting career that had seem him as both Opie on *The Andy Griffith Show*, and Ritchie Cunningham in television's *Happy Days*. Now he was firmly established as a director.

Parenthood, written by Babaloo Mandel and Lowell Ganz, who'd enjoyed a lengthy association with Howard, offered a top-notch list of names for its stars—Steve Martin, Mary Steenburgen, Jason Robards, Tom Hulce, and Dianne Wiest among the best known of them.

The film looked compassionately at four families, each headed by the offspring of a distant, alcoholic father (Robards). Gil (Steve Martin) was trying to be the perfect dad. His sister (Harley Kozak) was married to a man determined to turn their young daughter into a genius, at the expense of her childhood. The youngest son (Tom Hulce) was a ne'er-do-well, full of get-rich-quick schemes that never worked. And Helen (Dianne Wiest), the other sister, abandoned by her husband, was trying to be a good, liberal mother.

Helen was the one who experienced the greatest ups and downs. She'd ordered her daughter, Missy (Martha Plimpton), not to see her new boyfriend, Tod (Keanu). What she didn't realize was that, even as she spoke, the boy was hiding under the bed. And her son (Leaf Phoenix, younger brother of River) was acting very strangely, constantly locking his room and always carrying a grocery bag everywhere with him.

After Helen, purely by chance, came across some photographs of her daughter and Tod in bed, the girl ran away, only to return a few days later. Tod had been a jerk, she said, more concerned with his brothers and his fantasy drag racing career than with her.

What put a new spin on this turn of events was when Tod showed up on the doorstep to make up with Missy, and he happened to let slip that they were married. Helen completely changed her attitude. He was no longer "that Tod;" he was now her son-in-law, part of the family, even if he wasn't completely welcomed with open arms. He moved in, and Missy returned to high school.

And Tod proved to be the factor that brought her family together. When she finally discovered what was in her son's grocery bag—pornographic vide-otapes—it was Tod who talked to the boy and got to the bottom of the mystery. He became an older brother to the boy. And Helen found out that under the strange haircut Tod was really a sensitive human being, one who needed a real family after being abused by his stepfather. Things looked like they were going well until Missy happened to discover that Tod had abandoned housepainting (his brothers has taken off with all the gear) to fulfill his dream of drag racing.

Tod did race, once, and crashed. In the truck on the way to the first aid tent, Missy told him she was pregnant. And while Helen doubted the marriage would last, she felt they deserved whatever short amount of joy they could get from it.

In the end she might have been wrong. For, as she gave birth herself, having remarried, Tod, Missy and their baby were all together in the waiting room, with the rest of the family. And they all lived with a realistic amount of happiness ever after.

Parenthood achieved its moderate goal of being a bittersweet comedy with its feet firmly planted in everyday life. As *Newsweek* said, it was "part soap opera and part satire." And while it was rather obvious at times, telegraphing its messages as strongly as any television sitcom, there was plenty for any parent to relate to—the movie's exact intention.

Most critics enjoyed it. *New York* called it "surprisingly ambitious," with "gratifying reserves of emotion." *Time* felt that, "it really shouldn't work, but it does . . . there may be more good, solid performances in this unlikely context than in any other movie this year." And *People* raved that it was a comedy "with respect, insight, warmth and remarkably sustained wit . . . Here is one great American movie."

Only the *New Yorker* dissented from this overall view, finding it to have been "conceived generically, abstractly," and that its messages "all add up to a correct answer to the essay question 'What is Parenthood?' "

The truth was that the ensemble worked very well together in a way that more than did the material justice. The characters acted and reacted in perfectly natural, unaffected ways. At the end things were wrapped up too neatly, but the movie did give a sense of ongoing highs and lows, or, as *Newsweek* put it, "in the never-ending struggle of raising kids, the moments of peace and reconciliation can only be fleeting."

Although Keanu didn't have much screen time, he was once again in a pivotal role. Tod might have seemed flaky, but under that exterior was a heart of pure gold. He was the next generation edging into marriage and parenthood. And Tod was a natural parent, as his relationship with his young brother-in-law showed. Tod was a comic character, but only slightly more so than the others in the movie. There was the dark, serious underside of his own childhood, barely sketched in.

It was a fine line, balancing humor and sympathy, and to Keanu's credit, he trod it very surely. Perhaps it was odd to see him in a relatively small part immediately after a starring role, but it offered something different from his teenage characterization, an expansion for all those who'd discovered him in *Bill and Ted's Excellent Adventure*. Tod, although never more than on the periphery of the family, ended up as memorable as any of the main characters. That was a testament to the power of his acting.

But acting wasn't the only front where Keanu had been busy. It had kept him working, but he hadn't forgotten music. And finally he'd done something he always wanted to do—put a band together. They weren't ready to start playing gigs yet, but that was Keanu's long term plan.

He never wanted it to be more than fun. He wasn't looking for a record deal. He wasn't interested in trying to make a living at it. This was relaxation away from the pressure of business. But music was in his system, though, and it had to come out somehow.

"We're really bad," he told a reporter. And, for now, they were nothing more than a garage band, going under the name Dogstar.

"We play, like, folk music. Folk-thrash, maybe? But not quite thrash."

Of course, he knew the problems that would occur when they finally played. He wanted nothing more than to be the bass player, and maybe yell an occasional song. But, purely because of who he was, all the attention would be fixed on him. No one would care about the others, or even about the music. After band discussions and beers, they all decided it was worthwhile. They all wanted to play.

Being in the band grounded and exhilarated him in the same way that riding his Norton did. It was freedom, away from the hustle and schedules of movies. He could be a part of something, a cog or component, without having to stand out as the star. And the sheer physicality of the volume and the beat was a rush that left the adrenaline pumping just like a fast ride. So Dogstar was up and running, its practice and gig schedule wrapped around Keanu's work.

He still didn't own a house, although he'd made enough to buy one. He didn't even have an apartment, a place of any kind to call his own, but lived a curious, rootless kind of existence in a hotel. In fact, he didn't have much of anything. A couple of motorcycles, his guitars, some clothes and albums, and that was about it.

But for now he wasn't seeking roots. There was too much living to do to have ties. Keanu didn't have a girlfriend, and for the moment he wasn't looking for one. Getting dates was easy, if that was what he wanted. But there wasn't too much time for that any more.

He saw his mother and his sisters when he could. But trips to Toronto were becoming harder to arrange as he grew busier. And to have them visit, well, that wasn't easy, either, given that he had no real home base. But the love remained between them.

For the present, Keanu had plenty to keep him occupied. His diary was already full for the next year, with good, varied projects that would be taking him in a number of directions.

CHAPTER FIVE

The first thing on Keanu's calendar was a small part in *I Love You To Death*, which took him to Tacoma, Washington for location shooting.

The film starred Kevin Kline and Tracey Ullman as Joey and Rosalie Boca, the owners of a pizza restaurant. What Rosalie didn't know about her husband, though, was that he was a philanderer, a true Casanova, with an insatiable appetite for women. The hippie busboy Devo Nod (River Phoenix) who was her friend tried to warn her, but she wouldn't listen.

Inevitably, she found out. Distraught, she planned to kill him. After a number of hilariously unsuccessful attempts, she dosed his spaghetti sauce with sleeping pills. Once he was unconscious, Devo, who would do anything for Rosalie, would shoot him.

The problem was that Devo proved not to be a very proficient shot, wounding Joey only slightly. So Devo went hunting for his acquaintance Harlan (William Hurt), a stoned biker, and found him in a bar with his equally stoned cousin, Marlon (Keanu). After some brief haggling they agreed to do the job, but turned out to be every bit as inept as they appeared.

The police ended up investigating, the truth came out, and everyone ended up in jail while Joey recuperated in the hospital. But he realized the error of his ways, and that he truly loved Rosalie and wanted her back. So, as his act of atonement, he dropped the charges against everyone. And they all trooped off to live happily, and, in Joey's case, monogamously, ever after.

Murder might have seemed an dark, unusual subject for such slapstick humor, but *I Love You To Death* was a genuinely funny, offbeat movie that managed to pile up the laughs in an effortless manner. And as Harlan and Marlon, William Hurt and Keanu were the icing on the cake.

Hurt, a fine dramatic actor, didn't really have a history as a comic actor, but he proved more than adequate for the job, as the pair came across as a

Keanu in a scene from *Speed*, the hit film which catapulted him to superstar status. (Photofest)

With Ione Skye in *River's Edge*, where he portrayed a troubled teenager. (Photofest)

As Ted, with Bill (Alexander Winter) and Rufus (George Carlin) in *Bill and Ted's Excellent Adventure*. (Photofest)

Alongside the late River Phoenix in Gus Van Sant's controversial film, *My Own Private Idaho*. (Photofest)

Keanu as undercover FBI agent Johnny Utah, with Patrick Swayze in *Point Break*. (Photofest)

With Gary Oldman in a scene from *Bram Stoker's Dracula*.
(Photofest)

Accompanying
actress Sofia
Coppola to the
Independent Spirit
Awards in Los
Angeles. (© Frank
Trapper/Sygma)

Signing autographs at the Manitoba Theater Center before a performance of *Hamlet*. (© Marc Gallant, *Winnipeg Free Press*/Sygma)

With his sister Karina at the premiere of *Much Ado About Nothing*. (© Celebrity Photo Agency/All Rights Reserved)

A tense moment with co-star Sandra Bullock in *Speed*.
(Photofest)

Enlightened in Bernardo Bertolucci's *Little Buddha*. (Laforet/Premiere/© Gamma)

With screen love interest Aitana Sanchez-Gijon in *A Walk in the Clouds*. (© Gamma Liaison)

Keanu in the futuristic thriller *Johnny Mnemonic*.
(© Liaison Agency)

Keanu and his band, Dogstar, playing at Irving Plaza, New York. (Gene Shaw/Star File Photo)

wasted mixture of Laurel and Hardy and Abbott and Costello. Keanu, still wearing the partly shaved hairstyle he'd had in *Parenthood*, offered the perfect blank, unknowing gaze and stumbling walk of someone who'd spent years abusing his brain with all manner of legal and illegal substances. Their few stumbling minutes in the film were the highlights of a lovely little movie.

More importantly for Keanu, though, working on *I Love You to Death* introduced him to River Phoenix, who'd end up becoming a close friend. Keanu didn't really have friends in the business, preferring to keep work and social life separate, but in Phoenix he found something of a kindred spirit.

In some ways they were very much alike, with Keanu, six years the elder, acting as a kind of "older brother," as Phoenix once described it. The two of them had a great deal in common. Both had had unconventional childhoods (although Phoenix's was by far the stranger), and both were very serious about their acting. They were both musicians. And both had their wild sides.

For Keanu, that mostly meant riding on his motorcycle at night, his own way of looking death in the face. But that wild side could take other forms, as he told *Interview* in 1990.

"I want to be on speed!" he said. "I've never

been on speed. I want to be a speed freak for a while. Is that a stupid thing to say?"

Well, yes, it was a stupid thing to say, certainly in public. And it gave the indication that the dangerous edge might possibly spin out of control. In Hollywood, many things were readily available to someone with money and a recognizable name. Self-destruction was only a phone call away. It was always tempting. And occasionally he gave in.

"Keanu was as wild as anybody," said his manager, Erwin Stoff. "Like the rest of us, he experimented."

But the one place where Keanu was always totally professional was on the set. He was an actor, there to give a performance. More than that, he was a Method actor, which meant that when he worked, everything he did had to be in character. He literally became the person, even between takes, sitting in his trailer, or eating in the canteen.

And the next person he became was Martin Loader, with a gentle New Orleans accent, in *Tune In Tomorrow*. It was comedy again, but of a much different cut, adapted from Mario Vargas Llosa's novel *Aunt Julia and the Scriptwriter* by English novelist William Boyd. And it returned Keanu to the status of leading man

In its way, the movie was soap opera of the first

order, even as it parodied the genre. The intelligent, literate script had been what first attracted Keanu to the project. As Martin, he'd have a chance to play someone far less goofy than any of his recent film outings. Add to that Barbara Hershey and Peter Falk, two highly underrated American actors, in something that was decidedly left of center, and you had a film Keanu definitely wanted to be involved in.

In 1951, twenty-one-year-old Martin Loader was putting himself through law school by working part-time at a New Orleans radio station, WBXU.

His Aunt Julia (Barbara Hershey), who was technically not a blood relation, returned to town from New York with the intention of snagging a rich husband. She was older, sophisticated, and beautiful. Martin was smitten. Unfortunately, to her he was just a kid.

Meanwhile, at the station things were changing. A new scriptwriter, Pedro Carmichael (Peter Falk) was brought in to spice up the daily soap opera. So there were tales of incest, hidden pasts, and bizarrely evil Albanians making it compulsive listening.

Pedro, a man of the world, offered Martin his help in winning Julia's heart. But, even as he arranged trysts, he was copying down the words they spoke to use on the radio.

Then Julia dropped Martin. She had, it seemed, found herself a rich man. But Martin wouldn't give up so easily. A date in a nightclub became disastrous when Martin's parents arrived. He was told never to see Julia again. And she had disappeared.

But Pedro had it all under control. Even as his soap opera was reaching ridiculous levels, he was playing the real-life lovers like characters on the radio.

It all came right in the end. Pedro, having stirred up enough emotion with his plots to cause New Orleans' Albanian population to torch the station, also managed to reconcile Martin and Julia. As Pedro left town, they were making their plans to marry, move to Paris, and live together happily, away from prying relatives and interfering friends.

It was a wry, sweet comedy that entwined reality and fantasy in the manner of South American "magical realism." And it was a treat to see Keanu looking so clean-cut, with short, slicked-down hair. He was, in a way, the straight man of the piece, quite earnest about his love for Julia, but too innocent and open to be able to win her alone.

Vogue thought that what made the film such a "joyful romp" was "its optimistic embrace of the power of love," with the relationship between Martin and Julia being "one of the most oddly engaging screen romances of recent years." That, however, proved to be the only enthusuastic review. *People* was willing to call it a "pleasant distraction," faint praise indeed. But it was certainly better than the *National Review*, which found absolutely nothing to recommend in the film or the performances of its actors, feeling that Peter Falk's blatantly over the top, hammish excesses were "bovine." Even that was an improvement on *The New Republic*, which christened the production a "mess" and a "purported comedy . . . just a couple of sorry jokes."

Needless to say, these critics weren't bowled over by Keanu's work either, which was "unbelievably played" or "stolid . . . with the stunned expression of someone debilitated by his very first head cold"—words that were little short of stinging, although not as ugly as those thrown at Barbara Hershey, who was dismissed as "perennially juvenile and surgically rejuvenated. . . ."

It wasn't a movie that had crowds lining up around the block for tickets. But neither was it the disaster most reviewers made it out to be. It was a fairy tale of sorts, a fantastic one in every sense of the word, and needed to be seen as such. And Keanu's Martin was the innocent young man who wanted to win a fair lady, have his dream of becoming a writer in Paris come true, and live happily ever after—the very vision of youthful idealism.

Romance, and the pursuit of it, forced Martin to grow during the course of the movie, to quit dreaming and get on the beam.

"What appealed to me was [Martin's] spirit and his passion," Keanu said. "He's just about to break out of his repression." Which Martin did with resounding success, walking away from his family, his home, and a set career in the law—all for love.

If Keanu's New Orleans accent wasn't as thick and honeyed as it could have been, well, that was a minor fault. His portrayal of Martin, buoyed through the days by dreams and hope, was right on, and quite touching, as his innocence jarred heavily against the real world. There was a strong sensual element to the film, although Keanu said, "I don't see myself as sexy"—a judgment women around the world would disagree with. In fact, in rehearsal, he downplayed Martin so much that director Jon Amiel had to coax him into making the character "brasher and cocky." "He'd say, 'Smile at her, c'mon, you love her, make jokes.' " Which all helped. But the essential innocence remained.

After seeing him play flaky kids and stoners so

much, this role was, as he knew, a positive move for him. Martin was young, only twenty-one, and still at the mercy of his dreams, but he had at least one foot firmly placed in the real world, and the other was slowly, inevitably beginning to coming down. As the film's central character, Keanu really had to work, both to make Martin's behavior believable, and to break down the stereotype that was threatening to overwhelm him.

And this *was* work. Keanu had to carry the film—be its driving force—while acting alongside Barbara Hershey and Peter Falk, both strong personalities. After back-to-back supporting roles, not much more than a couple of weeks' work all told, this return to leading man was the ideal way to stretch himself.

Which Keanu did. He found the character's essential naivete and turned it into optimism. He took someone who could easily have been a guileless kid and made him into a man. But that was what he needed to do. He *needed* to move on, to open other things within himself. He needed to reflect on the fact that, at almost twenty-six, he wasn't a teenager anymore, but someone who was growing well beyond those adolescent parts.

After the filming was complete, he took off for a second session at Shakespeare and Company, the camp for actors in Lenox, Massachussets that offered intense workshops in the mechanics of acting, mostly breathing, and applied them to works from the Shakespearian canon. Although it was meant largely for those who worked on the stage—something Keanu hadn't done for a few years now—he still firmly believed the experience would give him something useful to add to his work. And it meant that for a while he could surround himself with people whose whole lives weren't dominated by screen appearances, or the hype, bull, and egotism of Hollywood. He could also work on his Shakespeare.

For Keanu had remained a staunch fan of Shakespeare, both as a reader and an actor. The plays contained every facet of the human condition and brillianty written words and roles that demanded, and often received, the best from actors.

"Shakespeare," he said, "is physically thrilling. It goes to my brain and into my heart."

Going to Shakespeare and Company was as much for himself as his acting career. It offered a depth, a centering, that movies couldn't. In Los Angeles he was on his way to becoming a star, albeit a very offbeat one who refused to follow the recognized path. But in Lenox he was just another actor, and was treated the same way as everybody else.

So, when the group produced *The Tempest* at the culmination of their study, Keanu was assigned a small clown role, something he enjoyed every bit as much as anything he'd done on film.

"There was a scene with my character and another character, Caliban . . . We get caught underneath this blanket, and we have this whole dance . . ."

It offered another challenge, forced him to get it right the first time—no retakes allowed. That was the only time he was truly happy, when the challenge was one he had to rise to and strain to achieve.

That was every bit as true for movies as it was for stage work. Anything less, while it might be fun, was simply reporting for work and earning a paycheck. Keanu would still give his best when it came to acting; the Method style that formed the backbone of his art wouldn't allow him to do anything less—but it was easy.

Still, movies were what he'd chosen as his main focus. His stature was growing, and he was a big star in the making. That meant that not all his choices could be artistic. Hollywood had perfected the art of the compromise. Keanu wanted a career, and that meant giving way sometimes, taking roles that he probably wouldn't have normally picked. The film industry ran on the bottom line of profit and loss, and that, as much or even more than performance, was what made stars. Once Keanu was fully established he could afford to indulge his artistic streak occasionally—at that point his name would even help bring people in to see a small film—but until then it was a case of taking the best parts offered to him.

And right now, that meant growing his hair again and becoming Ted Logan again for *Bill and Ted's Bogus Journey*.

CHAPTER SIX

It was the time when Hollywood went sequel crazy. If a movie did even reasonably well, a sequel was made, whether there was a story or not. *Bill and Ted's Excellent Adventure*, which hadn't been expected to set the world on fire when it was released, had been one of the sleeper success stories of 1989, largely due to word of mouth.

And so, inevitably, a sequel was ordered. Alex Winter was back as William S. Preston, Esq.. With his hair shaggy and unkempt again, Keanu returned to play Ted "Theodore" Logan. It seemed an odd, backwards step to make just as Keanu had begun to expand his range, especially as the aptly titled "Bogus Journey" wasn't very excellent to the people who spent money to see it.

Bill and Ted had finally graduated from high school, and were now sharing an apartment and working dead-end jobs. Their big hope for the future was still Wyld Stallyns, which now also included their girlfriends, the two princesses from fifteenth-century England. The band entered a contest, which, if they won, would bring fame, money and a recording contract. The only minor snag was that they still couldn't play.

Unbeknownst to them, far in the future a malevolent man was plotting to change history. He'd built "evil" Bill and Ted robots to travel through time and take the place of the real flesh and blood creatures, which they did by killing them.

It seemed like an abrupt ending, but the story wasn't over yet. It was just beginning. Bill and Ted were in a bad spot. A brief trip through hell was awful. Their only way back to life was to win against Death, which they did in a variety of games, including Battleship and Twister.

So, with the Grim Reaper as their new servant, Bill and Ted went to heaven, conned their way through the pearly gates, and found God. God directed them to the universe's greatest scientist, a Martian named Station, and the four of them returned to earth to bring Bill and Ted back to life, build "good" Bill and Ted robots to defeat the evil ones, and let Wyld Stallyns win the contest.

Picking up all their robot supplies at a large hardware store, they let Station work, and of course, he easily managed the simple task at hand. Evil was defeated, and Bill and Ted used the time machine to give themselves a chance to learn to play. So when Wyld Stallyns—now Bill, Ted, the princesses, and Death on bass—appeared, they were wonderful. And so they began to usher in a new era of peace and harmony for mankind through their music.

It was completely ridiculous, but then the first movie had been, too. That movie, however, had a freshness that was missing from the sequel. *Bill and Ted's Bogus Journey* just seemed stale and tired, as if the writers had been forced to rack their brains to come up with any ideas at all. It also lacked the ongoing sly wit that had made the original such a delight. Here Bill and Ted were simply a couple of airheads who happened to get lucky, nothing more or less.

Once again, and quite rightly this time, *People* could find nothing worthwhile in the film, saying, "... it only *seems* as if it takes three hours to get through," adding that the movies didn't "deserve to have cult followings ..."

The Nation, in an article on summer sequels, kept

its tongue firmly in cheek while discussing the film, stating, ". . . 'Bogus Journey' is the most ambitious work of the imagination that America has produced in recent years . . ." and pointing out that it was "a dudespeak translation of *Paradise Regained*."

In all fairness, the movie did have its humorous moments, even if they were few and far between, such as the games between Bill and Ted and Death, which parodied Bergman's *Seventh Seal* very effectively. Chess became Battleship, and Death turned into a poor loser, who insisted on the best two out of three, then three out of five, before finally conceding.

But the real fun, which had been so rich on the ground in *Bill and Ted's Excellent Adventure* was scarce here. The movie came across as a hurriedly written piece, more cobbled together than crafted, or, quite simply a vehicle to try and soak some summer money from theater audiences.

And neither Keanu nor Alex Winter looked too happy to be reprising their parts. The first time had been goofy, a great laugh, even if it had saddled them both with images that wouldn't go away. Bill and Ted, as *The Nation* said, were "useless role models for anybody—which is a large part of their charm"; here they couldn't even manage that dubious status.

This sequel was carefully marketed, with ads on television and a soundtrack album that was promoted in music magazines. But if the studio hoped it would have another big seasonal winner on its hands, it was mistaken. The kids—and they were the main audience for this—weren't fooled. As a money-making vehicle, *Bill and Ted's Bogus Journey* barely got out of first gear.

It was rather sad to see Keanu involved with the whole debacle. After starting to establish a real identity away from Ted "Theodore" Logan, it was a retrograde move to take part in this, especially, as *People* noted, his "main acting move [was] to nod vigorously."

As it was, his work came across as purely perfunctory. Keanu was never less than professional—pride wasn't about to let those standards drop, even here—but off the set he was very much himself, not the character, a certain sign that this time around he really wasn't into being Ted.

"He just has his own rhythm," was the way someone described it. Showing up for work in a skirt and combat boots appeared to be more a sign of not caring and asserting his individuality than anything else, although he claimed he made his dubious fashion statement purely because it was comfortable.

Still, craft saw him through the film. Even before
the movie was released, it seemed highly unlikely
there'd be a third episode in the lives of Bill and
Ted, for which many were grateful. And it left
Keanu free to move ahead with his career. Had *Bill
and Ted's Bogus Journey* been a success, the chances
of him ever completely escaping Ted would have
been minimal. As it was, the character would continue to haunt him for a few years yet, a ghost he
couldn't quite exorcise. But the roles he began to
get kept the shadows at a greater and greater distance.

After five comedies in a row, it was definitely time
for a change. And *Point Break* was that, a full switch
to an action adventure with a strong emphasis on
the action.

The role of Johnny Utah, a former college star
quarterback who turned FBI agent after a knee injury ended his career, held real appeal for Keanu.
As a clean-cut jock, and one on the side of law and
order at that, the part was about as far as he could
get from Ted Logan. It was a dramatic, intensely
physical part in a movie where right and wrong
wasn't black and white, but muted shades of grey.
And it gave him the chance to be paid to surf, a
sport he'd discovered after moving to California

and indulged in sporadically ever since.

Keanu still had real elements of the teen jock he'd once been. He continued to play ice hockey regularly and was a goalie in a league team. He rode his Norton everywhere, getting scrapes and scars from the accidents that happened from time to time.

By the time filming began, Keanu had been busy for several weeks in a gym working on his physique, to a very noticeable effect. Johnny was a jock, and a FBI agent at that, so Keanu had to look like one, too, with well-cut pecs and strong cop arms—the bulging biceps that looked so powerful onscreen.

Johnny had just graduated from FBI training at Quantico, number two in his class, and he'd been assigned to the bank robbery division of the Los Angeles office. His new partner, Angelo (Gary Busey), a twenty-two year veteran of the force and a bit of a renegade, had been working on a puzzling case for three years.

Bank robbers disguised in rubber masks of former presidents kept making their hauls. Each job was always professionally executed, with nobody hurt and nobody caught. They were still at it, and the FBI was no closer to catching them. The Ex-Presidents, as they called themselves, seemed to be untouchable, vanishing like ghosts.

Angelo had one clue—beach dirt. Added to the fact that the robberies only occurred in summer, he felt the bandits were surfers. And so he sent Johnny in undercover to infiltrate the surfing community.

First Johnny had to learn to surf, though, and with the help of a young woman, Tyler (Lori Petty), he mastered the basics. Through her he met Bodhi (Patrick Swayze), a man who sought the spiritual through danger—surfing, climbing, free-fall parachuting—the ultimate thrill. The two of them hit it off.

Eventually Johnny realized that Bodhi and his small group of friends had to be the Ex-Presidents. He tailed Bodhi, and noticed him casing a bank. So next day Johnny and Angelo staked out the place.

They almost missed the robbers. A car chase, then a foot chase, left Johnny close, but a jump blew out his knee. He could have shot Bodhi, but something held him back. Was it friendship?

The unspoken bond between Johnny and Bodhi grew until the end of summer. Then it was time for one last job before moving on. And to insure Johnny's cooperation, the Ex-Presidents had kidnapped Tyler, who'd become Johnny's girlfriend.

So he found himself involved in a robbery, caught on-camera without a mask. With Angelo's help, he tracked the gang to San Diego Airport. But it had become a bloody game. One policeman had already died. Now Angelo and a gang member were both shot, which left Bodhi, a wounded friend, and Johnny in a small plane heading for the Mexican desert.

The Ex-Presdients got away. Tyler was released, It was all over.

Or it should have been. But that winter Johnny caught up with Bodhi in Australia, after tracking him for months. He wasn't the neatly groomed rookie agent any more. His hair was long. He still carried a badge, but he was a surfer now. Bodhi was caught, and he knew it. The long game was over. The police were armed and waiting for him. He made a deal for one last ride on the biggest waves in the last fifty years, knowing there was no way Johnny could refuse him, and that he'd never come back.

Walking away from the beach, Johnny threw his badge in the ocean. Now it was really over.

As an action feature, it was perfect. Lots of heart-in-the-mouth stunts, some truly thrilling footage of both surfing and skydiving, and no shortage of suspense. But as anything more than mindless fun, well, it left a little to be desired. Any drama in the script was heavily overshadowed by all the movement, which tended to hamper the actors.

It was a big release. Keanu was an up-and-coming star, and Patrick Swayze had already made a big name for himself in films like *Ghost*, *Dirty Dancing* and *Roadhouse*. Although they'd both proven themselves popular at the box office, the critics hadn't exactly taken to either of them, which was reflected in the reviews of the movie.

Everyone was willing to concede that it *looked* wonderful, but beyond that they found little in the way of substance. "Pretty but dumb" was the way *Time*'s critique began, and that more or less summed up the general attitude. *Maclean's* found that two-thirds of the way through "the movie's frenetic pace and cliche heavy dialogue have become wearing," leaving the project "about as empty as Muscle Beach on a cloudy day." To *People* the film "doesn't have a brain in its gorgeous body." It was interesting that this particular movie was seen in the words many would use to describe a bimbo.

In all fairness, it was certainly true that there was more style than substance to the film, more stunts and sport than heavy acting. But it was easy to swallow at the level of pure fun and escapism, at which, *People* noted, it was "tough to beat."

But underneath all that, and behind the cliches

that filled out the writing, there was something interesting going on. As Tyler, Lori Petty (who would go on to star in *Tank Girl*) had a strong, assertive woman's role, even if it was undermined at the end. Swayze was convincing as a spiritual surfer even if—or perhaps because—some of his dialogue didn't make a whole lot of sense. But the biggest surprise was Keanu. Not only did he have a very buff body all of a sudden, but he had a new style.

Granted, Johnny Utah was all business, a graduate on the fast track to success, but even as he became distracted by Bodhi, there remained something very purposeful in Keanu's characterization. *People* might have found him "unconvincing as an agent as an ex-star quarterback," and *The New Republic* may have decided that he "evokes pathos just through his efforts to act," but in this movie he registered a very physical presence, more so than ever before. It was as if he'd finally discovered the star quality within himself that a few people had commented on and managed to draw it out. As the London *Observer* had noted of him, "When he's on screen, you watch him, however bad his acting may sometimes be."

But in *Point Break* his acting happened to be very good. The movie itself, while straining for something deeper, was really little more than summer fluff—but it did that excellently; it was escapism of the first order. And it showed Keanu in a completely different light. In addition to the comic with impeccable timing and the perennial teenager, he could really be taken seriously as an adult actor.

As a way of changing his screen image, *Point Break* worked exceptionally well. After the string of comedies it had been time to test himself again, to try and take his work to another level that would prove more satisfying to him in the long run.

And Johnny Utah was so different from the appealing flakes he'd been playing that the part was enough, at least for a while, to erase their memories. It was also a definite step forward from those performances that critics had liked to denounce as "one-dimensional"; Johnny had resonance, and while the script didn't allow Keanu to properly plumb his depths, he was able to show something of the man's complexity.

So now, having taken that initial step forward, he was ready to make a quantum leap. It wasn't one that would make him a full-fledged star, or even enhance his box office value all that much, but a very personal sidetrack into a small, strong film that would truly show exactly what he was capable of as an actor.

CHAPTER SEVEN

My *Own Private Idaho* wasn't an easy film on any level. Directed by Gus Van Sant, who'd achieved a level of success with *Drugstore Cowboy*, it was never intended to be simple entertainment. It achieved—or failed to achieve, according to some—that dubious state of Art. A curious, often downright bizarre mix of pseudo-Shakespearian and modern dialogue, it entwined the story of a narcoleptic street hustler with that of a son's wildness before assuming power from his father in a rather hallucinatory manner.

For Keanu this wasn't just a vehicle, this was something he believed in. And it gave him a wonderful opportunity to show his love of Shakespearian wordplay onscreen, in a setting that was utterly relevant to the modern world. And as an added bonus, it teamed him once again with his close friend River Phoenix.

Given the explicitly gay street hustling carried out by their characters, signing on for the film was a brave move for the pair of them. Both Keanu and Phoenix had established reputations as teen dreams. Their fans were primarily teenage girls, a fickle group at the best of times, and one easily lost because of something like this. But, artistically, this was something that just couldn't be turned down.

Phoenix played Mike Waters, an abandoned youth, a street kid, innocent, uneducated, lost, a narcoleptic who fell into a deep sleep during moments of stress and whose only way to make money was to work as a hustler. He made no distinction between men and women—in his world they were all just tricks. He drifted from place to place throughout the Pacific Northwest, looking in a half-hearted way for the mother who'd left him.

At a woman's house in Seattle he met Scott Favor (Keanu), another hustler, but one who was more self-possessed, self-assured and worldly. Scott was adamantly not gay, only sleeping with men for money. He became Mike's friend and protector, taking him to his home turf, Portland.

Scott was the son of Portland's mayor, just biding his time, and having his rebellion, until he inherited family money when he was twenty-one—a week away. Meanwhile he lived with the other street kids in an abandoned hotel, in a scene that coalesced around an aging, Falstaffian bum named Bob Pigeon (William Riechert). Scott loved and hated Bob, being kind, then robbing him.

But there was more living to do. Scott indulged Mike's dream of finding his mother, who'd left him years before. A motorcycle trip to Idaho to visit Mike's older, drunken brother offered a clue—a postcard from the place where she'd worked as a maid.

She was long gone by the time they arrived, with a forwarding address in Italy. Selling the motorcycle, they flew to Europe.

At the address, Mike's mother had vanished again, back to America. But living at the place was a lovely young woman, with whom Scott fell in love. He was about to turn twenty-one; it was time to renounce his misspent youth and live as an adult.

He took the girl back to America, leaving Mike with only a return airline ticket.

Making his way back to Portland, Mike was lost to the streets again—his only possible home—and back with Bob. They spotted Scott and his new wife emerging from a limosine and entering a fancy restaurant. Bob barged in and confronted him, but Scott quite bluntly refused to acknowledge the old man and had him thrown out of the place.

That rejection was all it took. Bob died. And, at the same time, so did Scott's real father. At the graveyard, while a somber service for the mayor was underway, a raucous wake for Bob Pigeon was conducted by the street kids.

Once again, Mike had lost his home. He was back on the road, going nowhere or anywhere, it didn't really matter—the same road, or another just like it, where he'd begun. He passed out. A truck stopped, and the occupants robbed him of his possessions and clothing, then drove off. Another car came along. It, too, stopped, and took him on board. Life went on.

It was Van Sant's vision, brought to life on what, for Hollywood, was the shoestring budget of $2.5 million. And, at best, it was a risky proposition, both commercially and artistically. As River Phoenix noted at the time, "Whether or not it works, it's a really noble try."

On balance, it was a try that succeeded. *My Own Private Idaho* attempted something rarely done in American cinema. It was a film that was deliberately nebulous, that had more texture and emotion than plot, a whole made up of contrasting parts.

Van Sant proved to be a relaxed taskmaster during the filming. On the set Keanu said of him, "Gus is really incredible to work with here . . . nonjudgmental . . . cool."

When not in front of the camera, many of the actors spent time at Van Sant's house outside Portland. Since both Keanu and Phoenix were musicians, and the cast also included Flea from the Red Hot Chili Peppers, jam sessions in the basement were a common event, often lasting until the early hours. It all helped make the shoot seem a pleasant, friendly affair.

That was probably just as well, given the intensity that Keanu and Phoenix had to bring into their roles. Neither was gay, and it became, said Van Sant (who was gay), "a political act to do a film like this. They're handling it very well for being obviously straight."

To research his role as Mike, Phoenix hung out with street hustlers in Portland. Keanu, too, looked at life out on the street, spending long nights on run-down street corners in Portland's Old Town. But when asked about his preparation, he said, "I didn't have to suck dick, if that's what you mean!" Indeed, in public he seemed a little defensive about the role.

"I'm not against gays or anything," he said, "but I won't have sex with guys. I would never do that on film. We did a little of it in 'Idaho' and, believe me, it was hard work. Never again."

Later, however, when the shooting was done, his outlook seemed to have lightened a little. He still openly declared in *Interview* that he wasn't gay before adding ambiguously, "But you never know."

But whatever baggage either of the stars might have brought to this movie, their work together elicited superb performances. And part of it was because of the friendship they shared in real life.

"River is my buddy, dude," Keanu said during an interview to publicize the movie. "I've always loved you, River. River is my best friend, and, to be honest, I don't have many of them."

The tenderness between them came across. Scott, the elder, looked after the person who'd become his charge as best he could, even though he knew he'd be leaving that life very soon. And he wasn't going to carry anything with him when he left. He was going to close his heart to the past and start afresh.

According to Van Sant, the movie was about "looking for a home. You may not find one, but you keep on looking." Scott always had one waiting for him.

But the film was also, in part, an appropriation of the Prince Hal story from Shakespeare's *Henry IV, Part I.* The idea wasn't quite as odd as it might have seemed. The comparisons between Hal and Scott were obvious (and highly played up). And it was done in a remarkably tongue-in-cheek manner. There were Falstaff billboards in the background, and the characters drank Falstaff beer. It was good fun, and, in its own quiet way, rather self-mocking, sounding important and portentous to deflate any pomposity in the film.

When the filming and editing were complete, what Van Sant had was nothing less than an artistic tour de force. It was giddy, even trippy in places, but the humanity, and the director's compassion for his characters, particularly Mike, the sad center of the film, was quite obvious. What he ended up with was something that was part road movie, part coming of age film, and part documentary. But the three gelled well into one strange, compatible whole.

Most critics saw it as a partial triumph, a very brave attempt that didn't always succeed. *Rolling Stone* called it "an exhilarating and challenging ride," while *Newsweek* concluded that it was "a far cry from seamless, but I would gladly trade a dozen well-made studio movies for one of its vital parts." To *New York* it was "disorderly . . . also a tenderly comical and beautiful piece of work . . . for all its messiness, it has the poetic faith . . ." although the magazine felt "the Shakespearian high spirits just don't fit the comic-bedraggled hustler milieu." *The Nation* described it as "a deeply moving film about unrequited love, abandonment, poverty and loss, realized with a gaiety of invention and a lightness of touch." *Maclean's* saw it as "the art film equivalent of a rainbow-layered cocktail— gaudy, outrageous and intoxicating" before summing it up as "a cinematic detour worth staying awake for."

In the *Library Journal*, the movie was taken as, "A harsh, raw, disturbing, and often beautiful film . . . highly recommended for its singular—though not always perfectly executed—vision."

But while most of the critics were able to find plenty to praise in the movie, there were, of course, dissenting voices. *Time* called it "essentially inert" with a "nonstory." And *People* went even further, saying it had "so many tiresome, pretentious scenes that it begins to look as if Phoenix's narcolepsy isn't part of the plot."

My Own Private Idaho was never meant to be a multiplex movie with vast weekly grosses. Even with such a pair of up-and-coming box office draws like Keanu and Phoenix, that was just never part of the equation. The film's subject matter was too marginal to ever attract big audiences. It was an art house film, pure and simple.

The reviews had made that abundantly apparent, even if it hadn't been before. The populist magazines, like *Time* and *People*, came down against it, while those inclined to the artier side found an element of confused joy in the picture's meanderings. Indeed, one publication offered a three-page review by a clinical psychologist that attempted to explain the actions and motivations of the characters.

But having cost so little to make, it didn't need to bring in a fortune to be profitable. And, perhaps unsurprisingly, it proved to be popular with the gay audience, some of whom quite vocally believed that Keanu and Pheonix had to be gay because it was the only way they could have achieved so much depth in their performances.

My Own Private Idaho brought Keanu into the public eye as a true, serious actor. With the less sympathetic lead in the film, he had to show some reserve, and never be willing to give all of himself to anything, while Phoenix was able to submerge himself completely in the lost youth that was Mike.

Both were very justly praised for their performances. *Newsweek* called Keanu "a good naturalistic actor," while in *New York*, he was characterized as "a graceful and wily actor with a sense of vagrant hauteur about him—he's singularly self-possessed." In *The Nation*, his portrayal of Scott Favor was viewed as "more of a star turn, which is appropriate for Scott's character. Even in his most intimate moments, he has a late-adolescent self-consciousness." *Maclean's* felt Keanu had "a disturbing talent for playing shallow characters . . . he is well cast an an opportunist who conducts his life as a series of poses." *National Review* summarized both lead performances as "fine."

Which they were. River Phoenix won the Best Actor Award from the National Society of Film Critics for his role as Mike. Keanu might not have carried away any trophies, but he did win the critics' respect, a less tangible but more enduring reward. After several years of being dismissed as a fairly lightweight actor, one whose range was thought to be very limited, the great notices came as an excellent vindication of his real talent.

With this and *Point Break*, it was perhaps possible that Keanu could leave his incarnation as Ted Logan behind. At twenty-six it was definitely time to make a break with juvenilia. Scott Favor was, at least, someone moving quite consciously and deliberately into adulthood, leaving his adolescence behind him like a shed snakeskin. And for the moment it looked as if people would be willing to let Keanu do the same thing.

As he'd emerged from his shaggy haircuts into someone sleeker and more stylish—whether that style be jock or hustler chic—it had become very apparent to more people that Keanu was a remarkably good-looking man. *Point Break* had played that up, and so, in a lesser way, did *My Own Private Idaho*. He was moving from teen idol to true Hollywood heartthrob.

It was ironic, really. He'd been so dedicated to the art of acting, to expanding himself in roles, to using the Method school to completely immerse himself in characters, and now his main recognition was coming from photographs in magazines.

To be fair, he would never have come to lead roles in movies at all without being photogenic and good-looking—that was a virtual prerequisite of the American system—but to find himself as a part of the pinup syndrome was definitely an odd turn.

But perhaps it shouldn't have been completely unexpected. His looks were intriguing and beguiling. With a strong facial structure, he was quite recognizable and distinctive, and more than pleasant to look at. The very slight Asian tilt of his eyes helped to set him apart from the whitebread American mainstream. It offered a sense of mystery, of the unknowable, an enigma that left questions.

Also, beyond any doubt, he had charisma. That had become properly evident in *Point Break*, and was confirmed in *My Own Private Idaho*. When Keanu was onscreen, the viewer's attention was riveted on him. And now that there seemed to be a new seriousness and purpose about what he was doing, the goofiness left behind, it was even more apparent.

Away from the set he remained an odd character, still very much the loner, fairly anti-social in a very social business. While other actors his age were in long-term relationships, he had no real girlfriend, just occasional dates that never seemed to pan out into romance. About the only things that really seemed to interest and occupy him away from work were riding his Norton, playing with Dogstar, and reading.

He had still to establish himself in any permanent residence, although he could easily have afforded to take the traditional Young Hollywood route and bought a house up in the hills. But hotel rooms were ample for his needs. He only needed place for his clothes and the books he was going through at the time. He seemed to be deliberately kicking out against the stereotype of success, and the idea of putting down any kind of roots.

The false bonhomie of being seen out at lunch and dinner in the right restaurants, talking to the right people, obviously meant nothing to him. And why should it? He was an actor, not a celebrity.

A career, as such, was unimportant to him. He wanted longevity, the chance to keep acting, to keep growing and challenging himself with different characters, not experience the mercurial rise and slow fall that happened to so many "stars" in the movie business.

Keanu was a man who was concerned with something that seemed rather quaintly old fashioned in the wheeling and dealing that created film hits—art.

He'd approached his most recent roles with great earnestness and energy, an overwhelming desire to make Johnny Utah and Scott Favor living, breathing, believable people. He'd succeeded, and in doing so, he had been able to reinvent himself as an adult. It was, all in all, a remarkable achievement.

The question was, could it possibly be enough? *My Own Private Idaho* was, by industry standards, a small film. But it was widely noted. And, after *Point Break* and the increased female attention

Keanu was receiving, the media machine had started to grind. It was as if now that he was a heartthrob, he had to become a star, never mind that in terms of billing he was one already. Sooner or later there would have to be a big budget extravaganza that would make him a virtual household name.

For now though, that wasn't on the horizon, and Keanu could just be himself, working in the way he wanted, attempting new things. And if he failed in them, that wasn't the end of the world. At least he'd tried, and done something he hadn't done before. There was every bit as much to be learned from failure as from success. The only difference was that for someone in the movies failures could become glaringly public.

With *My Own Private Idaho* out of the way, a picture that had been emotionally draining, it was time to move on to fresh pastures, and respond to an offer from director Francis Ford Coppola. Coppola had achieved a special niche in American filmmaking as someone who could reconcile art (*Apocalypse Now*)and commerciality (*The Godfather* series), even if his work often suffered from wild inconsistencies in quality. To be asked to work with him was something of an honor, and seemed like a sure sign of recognition for Keanu's own talent.

Unfortunately, that wasn't quite the case; Coppola's own motivation for casting Keanu in his new project was rather more mercenary than that. According to *The New Republic*, "he wanted a heartthrob who would draw young women."

Still Keanu went along with it. It would be interesting to work with someone so highly regarded. And Coppola had assembled a team of very talented players for his new movie—Anthony Hopkins, Winona Ryder and Gary Oldman—as well as musician/actor Tom Waits. At the very least it promised to be interesting.

CHAPTER EIGHT

The project was an extravagant remake of *Dracula*, to be grandly called *Bram Stoker's Dracula* because, as Coppola insisted, his version would be far closer to the original novel than any other that had been filmed. At least, that was his intention. Whether it ended up that way was a matter of conjecture.

Count Dracula (Gary Oldman) had been a hero in the Transylvanian fight against the Turks, winning tremendous victories. Returning home to celebrate, he discovered that his young wife, Elizabeta, had been told he was dead, and had thrown herself from the castle battlements, her heart broken.

Grieving, Dracula rejected God. His curses

caused blood to pour from a crucifix. He drank it, condemning himself to eternal life.

Five centuries later, in London, a solicitor's clerk, Jonathan Harker (Keanu), was dispatched to Transylvania to aid the Count with his purchases of English land. A dutiful young man, he said farewell to his fiancée, Wilhelmina (Winona Ryder), and traveled east.

The Count seemed a strange man indeed, and quite taken with Harker's picture of Mina (who strongly resembled his adored Elizabeta). But the business was transacted, and the Count made his odd preparations for his journey, even as he insisted that Harker stay longer; there was more business to be done.

In London, the now-youthful Count pursued Mina, after making a vampire out of her friend Lucy. The strangeness of her case attracted Dr. Von Helsing (Anthony Hopkins), who immediately recognized the problem.

Harker, meanwhile, was being subject to all manner of supernatural tortures. Eventually he managed to escape, his hair grey, and made his way home, joining the others in chasing Dracula. Except Mina, who'd come to the realization that Dracula was the man she loved.

The group followed Dracula back to Transylvania, determined to rid the world of this evil, and almost managed it, badly wounding him before moving in for the kill.

It was Jonathan who held the others off. He still loved Wilhelmina, even if her affection had gone elsewhere, and he understood that she would do what was necessary out of love.

Which she did, plunging the knife all the way through his body, before using the blade to cut off his head. The spell he'd put her under vanished. But the love remained, even when Dracula's curse was lifted from the world.

Visually, the movie was a sumptuous production, dark and dangerous, beautifully photographed and lit, with wonderful—although sometimes highly unlikely—costumes. Dracula's shadow could wander separate from him in the candlelight in a marvellously menacing way. It looked great.

But for all the glitz and grandeur, it was nothing more than an elegant failure, a true case of style winning out over content. As one reviewer noted, "This baroque, messy movie resembles a box of chocolates left too long in the sun," while *New York* bluntly summed it up as "among the most boring movies ever made."

The film very desperately wanted to be erotic,

but rarely succeeded; bared breasts and suggestive writhing didn't necessarily mean eroticism. "Everything remotely sexual is so glitzily and consciously packaged that it all remains . . . distant from the viewer," Stanley Kaufmann wrote. All in all, *Bram Stoker's Dracula* had very little going for it, and was definitely hampered by a script that was little more than a string of cliches. *America*, though, was willing to allow that this version was "scary and funny, beautiful to look at and great entertainment." But that was one of the few critical voices raised in the film's defense.

The casting also left a lot to be desired. Gary Oldman made a delicious Dracula, at war with his own conscience at times. But his work was inevitably compared to Bela Lugosi's classic 1931 performance and suffered in the comparison, as anyone's would. And as Von Helsing, Anthony Hopkins managed some real over-the-top, scenery-chewing acting, with, as *The New Republic* said, "an errant accent but with some fiber and fun." But, by the standards he'd established, it was a fairly rote performance. The movie's standout, surprisingly, was Tom Waits, whose acting ability seemed to improve by leaps and bounds, and who, as Renfield, proved to be "surprisingly fine."

The biggest problems came with Winona Ryder

and Keanu. Keanu had been brought on board primarily to attract young women, and maybe it was thought that Winona would have the same effect on young men. Although they were both fine actors, they were horribly out of place in this film.

Mostly, the trouble was the accent. Wilhelmina and Harker were English, and the people playing them were quite palpably not English, however much they strained. Winona, attempting to be a straitlaced schoolmarm, came across as laughably haughty rather than prim, while Keanu's cautious Harker was more wooden than anything else.

It was as if the accent had put a straitjacket on his acting. Only when he forgot the accent and acted in a more neutral, natural voice did Keanu come alive—and that was something he was given few opportunities to do. At the film's climax, when he was willing to let Mina finish off the Count because he still loved her, the script offered him no chance to show his internal conflict; the moment just glided by.

He was, *The New Republic* decided, "like a quite nice high school boy in the senior class production." This was one of the kinder criticisms of his role. According to *New York*, he was "pale and lifeless, he looks like a ghoul, too, even though he's nominally the hero." *The National Review* thought he looked "befuddled, and delivers his lines in an electronically amplified whisper." *Maclean's* declared him "perennially flat . . . as if he had wandered onto the set of *Bill and Ted's Transylvanian Adventure.*"

It was a shame that came back to haunt him. And *People* also invoked that bit of the past in its review, saying that Keanu was "limited and stamped" by Ted Logan to the point where you could "practically hear him saying, 'Most excellent fangs, Drac dude.'"

That was plain silly. There was absolutely no similarity between the characters, and Keanu had traveled a long way from *Bill and Ted's Excellent Adventure.* Agreed, he wasn't very convincing as Harker. It was a role he'd attempted and failed, and he said as much himself when he admitted, "I didn't give a performance in that one."

But it was an honorable failure, an attempt to stretch himself further and do something different. One thing it certainly never brought to mind was Ted Logan, but quite the opposite. Keanu's portrayal of Harker showed that he was quite comfortable playing an adult. The gawkiness of youth, so evident in *Bill and Ted's Excellent Adventure* and *Parenthood*, had vanished. Never did you feel that this was an adolescent playing a grown-up. Keanu was most definitely a man now.

He was also a very tired one. In the four years since 1988, he had been in twelve films, which was a fairly staggering work rate, and one that had just become wearing. So, with *Bram Stoker's Dracula* out of the way, he took a break of sorts. At least, it was a break from making movies. There was still work; he was still putting himself in front of people. But this time it was as the bass player of Dogstar.

The band had kept going around Keanu's commitments, playing clubs like the Whiskey A-Go-Go in Los Angeles. Keanu's name alone assured them of gigs; no matter how good or bad they might be, people were going to come and see *him*. This time around he was going on the road to see them as the band, which included another actor, Robert Mailhouse, of the soap opera *Days of our Lives*, on drums. So Keanu headed east to take part in the day-long Metalfest in Milwaukee. It was an odd place for what he'd described as a "folk-thrash" band, but it was the perfect way to relieve all the pressures of acting.

"They paid for our flight and free beer, but we were not what they expected," Keanu recalled. "I guess they were into the Reeves thing." But he still enjoyed the day.

"There were some incredible bands—it was a

mixture of hard rock and Satan rock, perhaps. But we're a folk band. We should not have been there. They threw beer at us and told us to fuck off and [shouted] 'You suck!' It was beautiful. It made me laugh. I said to the guitarist, 'Let's do one of our Grateful Dead covers!' It was a glorious moment."

Music was an escape valve. On screen he was always someone else. In the band he was too, but in another way, appearing as a magnified version of himself. Playing a gig released all the tension inside. He could take it all out on the bass, get that immediate adrenaline rush, a reaction—be it good, bad, or indifferent—from the audience immediately, then let it all seep away later.

Much the same could be said of the sport he still took part in, ice hockey. Playing focused everything inside, then drained it later. And both music and hockey, in different ways, were very physical activities. So, too, was surfing, although Keanu's chances to do that were growing fewer and fewer. It was hard to just show up at the beach without being hassled by fans.

But that wasn't true of riding his Norton. On the bike he could disappear. Under a helmet and wearing shades he could be anybody; it offered the perfect anonymity. And once again, it was a very physical activity. The rider used every part of his body directly to control the machine. That contact had always been a part of his delight in riding. Unlike a car, it was more basic and open, the modern day equivalent of riding a horse.

Under the spell of the rush—whether it was playing bass, or playing hockey, or riding, or whatever—it was possible to put the real world aside for a while, and forget everything, which may well have been one of its attractions for Keanu.

But acting remained his main obsession, his vocation. Taking time off was nice, but as soon as the opportunity to work on something close to his heart occurred, Keanu jumped at the chance.

The project was a film version of Shakespeare's *Much Ado About Nothing*, directed by and starring Kenneth Branagh, the Englishman who'd made an international name for himself with his *Henry V*.

Keanu, of course, loved the flow of Shakespearian language, the machinations of plot, the piercings of the human condition. This was something he couldn't have said no to. And taking part put him among an elite of actors—Branagh himself, his wife Emma Thompson, Denzel Washington, Brian Blessed, and Richard Briers—giving him quite visible acceptance as a serious actor.

One of the Bard's great comedies, the play is a battle of the sexes, misled by dirty tricks, where simple fools help carry the day, and all ends happily. Branagh had worked extensively on the text, mostly pruning it to a movie length that left the story and the spirit intact. He'd kept the original Italian setting, but put it in an frame that deliberately never quite matched up with any specific historical time.

As Don John, the bastard brother of the Prince, Don Pedro (Denzel Washington), Keanu was the rotten apple in the barrel, trying his best to break up the romance between Claudio (Robert Sean Leonard), and Hero (Kate Beckinsale), before vanishing—only to be returned to face justice.

It was a splendid, sunny movie that managed to be great fun. Branagh and Thompson played their leads superbly, bringing the language alive, and making Benedick and Beatrice really spark off each other. As *The New Leader* noted, it was "immensely plush and glossy," while the *National Review* summed it up as "rollickingly extroverted . . . quickly converting its sounds of woe into hey nonny, nonny."

Others weren't quite so effusive. *Commonweal* held back, saying, "A great Shakespeare film? No, it hasn't got a majority of successful performances. But it does have what few Shakespeare films, what few movies of *any* sort, possess: zest."

The New Republic supported the film, calling it "a flawed gem. Certainly, regrettably, flawed; still, a gem."

Almost all the critics had some reservations about the production. And while the film did have its faults, as *People* noted, "a goofy montage of Branagh splashing wildly in a fountain while Thompson kicks up her heels on a swing. Ne'er hath romance seemed so much like unto a Doublemint ad," it was overall a very successful, entertaining interpretation of a difficult Shakespeare comedy, one whose darker edges could distract from the overall humor.

As Don John, Keanu didn't have a whole lot to do. Don John was primarily the catalyst, the one who engineered the lovers' trials caught in a mass of spite. And from his very first scene, Keanu let it be known that his was an extremely unhappy character. In the Italian sunshine, when everyone else was smiling and happy, he was the one with the permanent scowl behind his beard.

Ruining things for people by using his malice, that was his work. And only when that was done, as he left the villa, did he allow himself the malicious pleasure of laughter, as nasty as any villain in a Victorina melodrama. For a short moment you almost expected him to twirl his mustache.

Unfortunately, the reviewers seemed to find pleasure in finding his (and the other North American) performances sadly lacking in comparison to the English co-stars. *The New Leader* asserted that they "walked through their parts on what they hoped was a cloud."

The National Review was quite specific about Keanu's failings: ". . . undistinguished by verve, flamboyance, or mere individuality. His heavy-lidded eyes are usually at the same aperture as the mouth of a child being force-fed spinach, and he snarls his way listlessly through his lines."

Commonweal was no kinder when it said, "Keanu Reeves is quite bad as Don John. He holds onto one . . . note throughout and never shows us the villain's pleasure in his own malice."

The New Republic's assessment cut every bit as deep: "Keanu Reeves, as the villianous Don John, knows all his lines and gives the sort of performance that makes parents beam at college productions."

The Nation offered a slight, albeit tainted ray of hope when it called his performance "adequate," before adding, "and certainly more articulate here than in the Shakespearian sections of *My Own Private Idaho*."

All of this would have been fine and justified if

Keanu had played the Don John they were expecting. Instead, the character he portrayed was one who was largely cold and calculating. Still the Prince's bastard brother, he was full of resentment at having to defer to the true heir. His revenge was icy, not the fire the critics seemed to have been programmed to anticipate.

Given that, he executed his role perfectly. Keanu played a man consumed, but not by any kind of passion. That made his scowl and "heavy-lidded eyes" quite appropriate. He exuded menace. And he certainly held his own in such august company as Branagh and Thompson.

But why shouldn't he? Keanu had extensive experience with Shakespeare, from his teenage Mercutio to his two sessions at Shakespeare and Company. Of the non-English actors in the movie, he was probably the most familiar with the Bard, and one whose training had come closest to anything the esteemed Royal Shakespeare Company or RADA had to offer.

He was also someone who read Shakespeare for pleasure. He was familiar with the language, the meanings that had become hidden over four centuries, and the texts. The plays were one of the ongoing joys of his life.

No, here was an instance where the critics were

wrong. Keanu's portrayal of Don John hadn't been a failure. Quite the contrary. He'd handled things perfectly, and, similar to the other leads, put his own spin on the character. And he'd shown—to the satisfaction of many viewers and his peers, if not the critics—that he was more than capable of classical work.

As soon as the filming had wrapped, Keanu was preparing for his next role. This one was a move to an altogether higher plane, from the classics to the classical. Keanu was going to be Buddha.

CHAPTER NINE

At first glance Keanu seemed an unlikely choice to play Prince Siddhartha in *Little Buddha*. After all, this was a man who renounced worldly wealth to become an ascetic in the forest, the man known as Buddha, whose wish was to save the world from endless pain. Keanu might have gone his own way, but he wasn't generally described as unworldly.

He was even a little mystified by the casting himself. So when he first met director Bernardo Bertolucci, who'd won an Oscar for *The Last Emperor*, he asked him.

"He said it was my innocence," Keanu related later to *Newsweek*. But Bertolucci was unfamiliar with the *Bill and Ted* films, and the lingering impression they'd left of a lovable goofball who marched to a slightly different drumbeat.

"When I met him," Bertolucci recalled, "he showed me something very enigmatic. I discovered only recently this 'dude' thing. I was not considering this prejudice, especially in the United States, against Keanu Reeves."

Luckily, enough time had passed for most of that to dissipate, although bits of it would remain at the back of people's minds, particularly writers, who would use titles like *Goodbye, Airhead* and *Keanu's Excellent Adventure* in the future.

But the essential innocence Keanu often projected had remained intact, and was the kind of natural plaintive vulnerability that was a part of Siddhartha's makeup. In that regard he was perfect for the role. The major problem was that physically he looked too robust, too well-fed for a man living in the woods.

So he began to prepare for the role. He didn't go on a special diet to lose weight and end up with his ribs showing through his skin. His solution was faster, simpler, and probably more authentic. "Not eating," he said.

Throughout the filming he stayed in character, part of the Method to make the new persona a more realistic fit. He talked in an Indian accent, let his hair grow wild, and barely ate. In fact, Bertolucci wryly noted, the only time he returned to his regular self was "if there was any really good French Bordeaux around; then he was very keen."

Siddhartha was, without a doubt, a plum role in a film that would be artistically satisfying, even if it was unlikely ever to be an American box-office hit.

The movie offered two parallel stories, that of Siddhartha, the only son of a rich king who lived 2,500 years ago. At his birth feast, an old, revered hermit wandered into the proceedings and pronounced great things for the baby.

His father cosseted and protected him, and so Siddhartha grew into an innocent young man, married and became a father.

But the real world inevitably intruded. On a procession through town he saw two beggars, followed them, and his eyes were opened to all manner of human suffering. He knew what his mission was—to break the circle of life and death.

He left the palace, and his family, to become a wanderer—a pilgrim of sorts, seeking enlightenment, to become the Buddha.

This tale was interwoven with the story of Jesse Conrad (Alex Wiesendanger), a Seattle boy who, it was thought, might be the reincarnation of a Buddhist Lama. His father took him to the monastery in Bhutan, where the truth of the matter could be established.

He was in competition with two other children—until it was decided that the Lama had been reborn in all three. As the decision was reached, the monk who'd led the search died.

Back in Seattle, Jesse was out in a sailboat with his parents. His mother was now quite visibly pregnant. On the waters of Puget Sound, the boy let a bowl of the dead monk's ashes float upon the water. His decision about whether to spend his life in Bhutan could wait until he was older.

It was a sweeping, gorgeously made film, which was only to be expected from the director who'd made *1900* and *The Sheltering Sky*. And it was obviously a labor of love, a tribute to Bertolucci's own embrace of Buddhism.

At the same time, though, it was confusing. It didn't offer any vast spiritual insights, and its main tale, that of Jesse, seemed somewhat pointless, which became all the more apparent as the story progressed. The Siddhartha section, however, did offer real depth, to the point where it was possible to believe that Bertolucci might have done better to expand it into a whole movie.

The reviewers seemed equally baffled by the picture. All seemed to agree that it was visually stunning, but other than that, it was difficult to see a reason for it all. In *The New Republic*, Stanley Kauffmann called it "in dramatic terms, pointless, except for those camera banquets," which he likened to "*National Geographic* in action." *New York* found that Bertolucci was "left making pretty pictures—and whimsical jokes about the ineffable." Boyd Tonkin, writing in *New Statesman*, felt that it came across "as a budget-busting live-action Disney—a wholesome fairy tale about the strange ideas of some ordinary folk, taken from a book crammed with sumptuous photographs." The *New Yorker* summed it up quite simply as "never less than sumptuous, and never terribly interesting . . . Buddha was bold enough to see beyond beauty. Bernardo Bertolucci is trapped inside it, and he may never get out." *People* dismissed it quite easily with the idea that if you looked for substance in the things that were "polished to a uniform shine . . . you will probably lose your temper."

That might have been a bit of an exaggeration. While the point of the story might have been missing, its telling was always engaging enough, and the Nepalese scenery was breathtaking. Alex Wiesendanger was ingenuous as Jesse, a curious child who comes to understand more about the world, and it was a welcome change to see Bridget Fonda in something other than a frantic twentysomething role.

But the clear joy of the film was Keanu. Even the critics who in the past had had very little praise for his work saw that. *The New Republic* said he had done "tolerable work" before, "but here he carries off an extremely demanding role. Not for a moment do we doubt that he is an Indian prince . . . or that he goes through a spiritual struggle to become the Buddha," and that "he has found the center of the role. He has dignity, tenderness, poise."

The New Yorker thought that "the casting of Reeves as Siddhartha is the movie's one true inspiration," albeit feeling it necessary to qualify anything resembling outright praise of Keanu with "he may sound like Peter Sellers in *The Millionairess*, and the lines themselves come straight out of *Tommy*, but with this kind of ethereal nonsense you *need* a goofy hunk. Under the weight of a serious actor, things would have collapsed within minutes; as it is we can sit and enjoy Reeves enjoying himself, and think how great he looks with kohl-rimmed eyes . . . We still laugh at *Little Buddha*, of course, but Keanu helps us laugh along with it, and not just cackle in its face." Perhaps it was something less than his performance really merited, but it was kinder than the reviewers had been in the past. It was a start.

Needless to say, though, those views hardly represented everybody. The critics were just starting to come around to his side; it would have been to much to find them united behind him already. *New York* definitely wasn't crazy about Keanu's portrayal, finding it as if he went through "the three phases of what appears to be a pretentious magazine spread," and then, as the Buddha, "Reeves looks like a bulimic model." The *New Statesman* summed him up as "impassive," and left it at that.

Keanu might not have been perfect here, and maybe not even as good as he had been in other parts, but he was able to bring the role that something unusual it needed to succeed—a laid-back charisma. At first, his skin darker, eyes outlined in kohl to accent their unusual shape and angle, and a cascade of curls falling onto his back, he didn't even look like Keanu.

And later in the movie, when the face was more obviously his own, he was able to transmit something quite abstract—the Buddha's detached bemusement at life. Keanu utterly believed himself in the role of a man who had gone from worldy wealth to spiritual wealth, and the majority of the audience believed along with him.

Little Buddha marked the real turning point in his relationship with the film critics. While there'd been the occasional strand of praise before, now some of them, finally, were willing to take him seriously as an actor and acknowledge that he had a talent that went beyond saying "Dude!" and "Excellent!" That in itself was a worth celebrating.

The reality was that over seven years he'd proved himself capable of almost anything. His comedy work had been impeccable, with a natural sense of timing and slapstick. His dramtic work on screen, right from his first moment in *River's Edge*—with the exception of *Bram Stoker's Dracula*—had never been less than compelling. Plenty of people understood that; it was why many saw him as one of the most talented actors of his generation. Now, with the critics being willing to forget *Bill and Ted*, and recognize some of his qualities, he'd fully broken through.

In some minds he'd been a star for quite some time. Now, it seemed, he was finally on his way to breaking through into the mass consciousness as someone other than a goofball teenager.

It should have been a good time for Keanu. But instead, circumstances turned it into something very sad. On October 31, 1993, River Phoenix collapsed outside the Viper Room, the Los Angeles club partly owned by actor Johnny Depp. Less than an hour later he was dead at twenty-three. The post mortem showed toxic levels of cocaine, morphine, and valium in his bloodstream.

Keanu and Phoenix, of course, had been friends since meeting on the set of *I Love You to Death*, and became much closer as the co-stars of *My Own Private Idaho*. Their common interest had been acting, but quickly extended to music. Keanu had Dogstar, while Phoenix played guitar and sang in his own band, Aleka's Attic. Both were part of the post-punk generation for whom music was every bit as important as movies. Picking up an instrument seemed as completely natural as acting, in some ways even more so, because it gave them a chance to express *themselves*, rather than take on a character to utter someone else's lines.

The pressures of work kept them from seeing each other much, but the affection between them remained. Phoenix's death came as a blow to Keanu. As he said, it "scared the hell out of" him. "I think of it as an accident," Keanu said. "I can't make sense of it."

Expressing his feelings about it was difficult. The emotions were there, bottled up inside; articulating them was much harder.

"I was terribly, terribly sad," he told *US*. "Incredibly sad. And, um, I miss him very much."

Keanu's life was undergoing some changes. Poor River was gone, one of the few friends he'd had in the business. The press was beginning to take him seriously. Even academia was staring at him. At the Art Center College of Design in Pasadena, instructor Stephen Prina had begun a course on the films of Keanu Reeves. On the surface, the course could have been taken as one of those very California types of jokes, but Prina was deadly serious. This wasn't an easy course, or a setup for a quick credit and a good grade. Instead it used Keanu as a means for analyzing modern film and contemporary culture, focusing not only the movies he'd made, but also the philosophical texts of Michel Foucault and others, and showing the place they all took in modern life.

It was hardly no-calorie popcorn fare. Instead, it was three months of very solid work. And it made Keanu the first of the younger generation of Hollywood actors to have a course taught about him, which perhaps offered him some small measure of satisfaction for having been the butt of critics' scorn for so long. But the honor was more than justified. Of all the actors in "Young Hollywood," Keanu, more than any of the others, stood outside the pack. He went completely his own way, demonstrating a much wider—and more daring—range than any of the others. Yes, he was handsome in that familiar movie star way, but he was also well-schooled in all aspects of drama. This wasn't just a road to a six-figure salary and billing above the title for him. This was Art. It was inside him; he had no choice but to do it.

That was why he was willing to take chances, to play the unsympathetic Scott in a film like *My Own Private Idaho*, or Siddhartha, roles that truly stretched him and involved him in quality productions, when he could just as easily have been taking the lead in some major studio blockbuster. It simply wasn't about the money, which was true of many people his age all across the world.

It was the time of the slacker generation—Generation X—or whatever name was currently in vogue. The kids who'd been alienated teenagers in the '80s had grown up, left school and college, and moved on. But all those old American dreams that had been programmed into them had vanished. Work was something that had to be done to pay the bills. Beyond that it had very little value. Other things were more important. Fun. Friends. Art.

So it was natural that they would relate to an

actor in their age group who didn't compromise, but followed his heart into projects. Nor, really, did it hurt that he'd played Ted Logan, a sort of icon of their high school years. The critics might have just begun to view Keanu in a friendly light, but his core audience had been doing so since the time of *River's Edge*. He was one of them. They understood him all too well.

Given his friendly relationship with Gus Van Sant, it wasn't too surprising that Keanu agreed to become involved with *Even Cowgirls Get The Blues*. The movie, adapted from Tom Robbins's counterculture bestseller of 1976, featured Keanu's name high on the cast list, but in truth his part was little more than a cameo, less than five minutes on screen and a line or two of dialogue—perhaps two or three days' work.

In some ways the movie closed a circle that had begun with *River's Edge*. There he'd played against Crispin Glover's manic character as a sort of sidekick. Here, Glover played his assistant. And one of the film's stars was Rain Phoenix, River's sister. Keanu, of course, had worked with both River and Van Sant on *My Own Private Idaho* a couple of years before.

But even with that small weight of history, you

had to wonder exactly what Keanu was doing here. Playing a very successful Native American watercolorist, hiding behind bushy sideburns and a tartan tuxedo, his character became the victim of an asthma attack upon meeting Sissy Hankshaw (Uma Thurman), the hitchhiker with the outsize thumbs. It was a role that demanded very little of him. In fact, as the movie progressed to a very different story, the question arose: Was Keanu just part of the confused plotting of the film, or just cynically added in to lure people into the theaters?

In the end, it really didn't matter; no one could be sure in the mess the movie became. Even several months in the editing room couldn't save the picture from being a disaster, as the critics all seemed to agree, the comments ranging from "half-cooked" to "bubbleheaded cuteness," leaving everyone to hope that next time out Van Sant would return to something of substance.

While Keanu was already a star in some circles, he still hadn't broken through to mainstream audiences. His name was known, of course—he'd been in too many movies for it not to be—but his image remained a little left of center, out on the fringes. And that was fine. He was working flat out, as it was. He didn't need mass adulation to know when he'd done good work. And he wasn't really concerned about whether or not he would find it in his next venture.

He'd done the action/adventure genre before, with *Point Break*. But this movie offered him something different, a blunt SWAT team cop called Jack Traven whose straightforward manner could have come from *Dragnet*. It was a good script, with plenty of humor, and even some romance. Its title was *Speed*.

CHAPTER TEN

His preparation for *Speed* brought Keanu two things—bulging biceps and a new haircut. It was, quite literally, a big change from the skinny, religious Siddhartha, one that Keanu managed by spending six days a week in the gym for a month and a half, strenuously lifting weights.

"I wanted to have cop arms—big, beefy," he told *Newsweek*. And he got them, they strained against the sleeves of his T-shirt. The haircut, short, cropped to little more than a crew cut really, utilitarian, businesslike, the perfect 'do for a man of action.

From ancient India to modern Los Angeles, from a man who sought "the Middle Way" to one who resolved crises, even down to the physical appearances, the change was almost schizophrenic, as extreme as it was possible to get. That Keanu managed to pull it off as successfully as he did was a strong testament the maturity of his ability.

Jack Traven wasn't Johnny Utah. Where Johnny, still a rookie, allowed himself to get emotionally involved in his case, Jack was a veteran, a SWAT officer, detatched, always weighing his options, and trying to think several moves ahead to outguess his opponents.

Speed began dramatically, with a hostage situation. Jack and his partner, Harry Temple (Jeff Daniels) were able to foil it, but not catch the perpetrator.

The job was only just beginning, though. The man who'd got away wanted revenge on Jack. And he got it by booby-trapping a bus. Once it reached 50 miles an hour, if the speed dropped below that mark, a bomb on board would explode.

Jack managed to board it on the freeway. After the driver was disabled, a young woman, Annie (Sandra Bullock) took over the wheel, while Jack's SWAT team colleagues caught up to them.

Diverted onto an open freeway, things looked hopeful, especially when they reached the airport, with a road around the runways that they could circle. Jack tried to disarm the bomb, but couldn't.

Eventually the bus passengers were evacuated. Only Annie and Jack were left. The steering was set, the gas pedal pushed down, and they escaped, leaving the bus to crash.

But the police still had to catch the criminal, a former cop (Dennis Hopper). He was clever, managing to evade them, and, on the way, take Annie as a hostage, forcing his way onto a test run of the new subway.

Jack gave chase and managed to get in the car, fighting the bomber as the train gained speed on the track.

Of course, the good guy won. The criminal was decapitated, and Annie and Jack ended up in a warm embrace. It looked like the start of a beautiful friendship.

Released in June 1994, it was the perfect summer movie: lightweight, but with enough twists and turns to keep the audience on the edge of their seats. Without being an out-and-out comedy, it managed nearly as many laughs as it did thrills, letting the characters stay very human and down to earth. And however much Jack Traven tried to carry himself like a machine or an android, the man lurked close beneath the surface.

Of course the studio expected, and fervently hoped, the movie would be a hit. They had a substantial amount of money invested in it; at a cost of $41 million, it was hardly a small film. But even they were unprepared for the way it took off. *Speed* took in a stunning $85 million in two months and finished the year with a gross of more than $105 million in the U.S. alone, placing it firmly in *Variety*'s top ten box office hits for the year.

Nor was it just the crowds who loved this one. For once, audiences and critics were united in their enjoyment of a film. The *National Review* began its criticism with the words, "At last an action picture out of Hollywood that satisfies," and continued, "Of course, nothing about *Speed* can be taken seriously; it is lightweight stuff." Even so, it remained thoroughly pleasurable. In *New York*, David Denby declared it to be "a movie that hits the summer season jackpot," adding, "*Speed* is not a chase, but a ceaseless hurtling projectile, a virtuouso machine-poem of force." He, too, happily pointed out that the film had "no social point to make," feeling that, "for once, this action-film blankness is a boon," and finally concluding that it was "brainless, relentless, and almost always overwhelming." To *Newsweek* it was "real escapism," a movie that was "one likely blockbuster that doesn't feel too big for its britches. It's a friendly juggernaut."

The New Yorker, after listing *Speed*'s faults ("bare

of emotional development," "characters . . . no more than sketches," "addresses no social concerns," "morally inert") turned around and quite bluntly pronounced it "the movie of the year." Comparing it very favorably to three titans of the action genre, *Die Hard, Terminator,* and *Alien,* Anthony Lane finished by remarking, "The movie comes home in triumph, and we go home in shreds. It was never a contest . . ."

For *Variety,* "*Speed* . . . manages to deliver the goods as a non-stop actioner that scarcely pauses to take a breath," and in *Time,* Richard Schickel found that "the film's sheer cut-to-the-chase straightforwardness is part of its appeal . . . executed with panache and utter conviction."

Rolling Stone called it "action movie heaven," and ended by declaring, "*Speed* cinches its spot as the thrill ride of the summer by providing characters to hiss at and root for . . . two hours of pure pow without gratuitous gore . . . *Speed* works like a charm." Even *People*'s summation was short and sweet: "*Speed* is worth the ride."

Of course it was pure escapism, a popcorn movie. It had no pretensions of being anything more. Like a big blockbuster novel to take on vacation, the film never pretended to be anything but entertainment, the perfect way to pass a couple of hours. And it succeeded. It was a white-knuckle ride that never took itself too seriously, the type of movie that made you laugh even as you were gripping the arms of your chair.

And yes, it followed completely in the footsteps of the genre. But the cliches it borrowed—and there were a few—were tweaked very neatly in this film; director Jan De Bont had worked as a cinematographer on *Basic Instinct* and *Die Hard*. Those films both knew what they were doing. Indeed, *Die Hard* was something of a model for *Speed*.

"When we were working on the writing," said screenwriter Graham Yost, "we kept *Die Hard* in mind."

Unlike that film, though, *Speed* wasn't littered with corpses, a point definitely in its favor with the public. Yost hadn't even wanted to include the sequence at the opening of the movie where Hopper stabbed a security guard in the ear with a screwdriver.

"I argued against that," he said. "For me it set a slightly wrong tone for the film, although it does establish that this is a very bad guy."

But *Speed* really didn't need a body count in the dozens or hundreds. It offered a hero who didn't have to keep killing people to prove himself or achieve his objective. And it built up the drama through a number of small incidents. That was one of its strongest points, but also one that could also have easily killed it at the box office. Did America want tension, or, in its heart of hearts, did it want corpses strewn all over the scenery? De Bont, and Twentieth Century Fox, who financed the film, were betting on the former.

In truth, *Speed* was a very expensive gamble from the beginning. It was Yost's first feature script, and De Bont's directorial debut. Keanu had been in one action picture, but it hadn't done especially well, and he didn't exactly seem like a typical action hero. And even though his co-star, Sandra Bullock, had been in feature films before, including *Demolition Man* and *The Thing Called Love*, she was an unknown quantity to most people.

But as Annie, Sandra Bullock came very close to stealing the picture from Keanu. She managed to exude a sparkling mix of the brash and scatty, a thoroughly modern version of some 1930s movie heroines. The chemistry between Annie and Jack was always evident but understated, an extra ingredient in a film that simply barreled along, a juggernaut that easily rolled over almost all the summer competition.

It had all the elements—Dennis Hopper playing the type of role he virtually could have patented as a scenery-chewing mad bomber, non-stop action that piled thrill upon thrill until it seemed that it couldn't possibly get any higher. The bus was the centerpiece, of course, but the scenes that surrounded it in the elevator and the subway also managed to build tension to almost intolerable levels, making *Speed* something close to three films in one.

All in all, it had everything going for it.

And for once, the critics even admired Keanu's work in the film as much as they enjoyed the movie itself. There was a distinct irony in that playing Jack Traven, who for most of the film emoted so little, didn't really require the complex skills and experience Keanu had brought to, say, *My Own Private Idaho*.

The *National Review* gushed over him as "... an intense face with lean, limned features ... isn't half bad on the big screen ... Here his close-cropped hair and sharply etched countenance, abetted by lithe, pantherish movements, stand him in good stead. Though a young man of action, he manages to look intermittently thoughtful ... Concerned but unsentimental, relentless in a good cause ..." They were words that came perilously close to the area of film fandom.

New York's David Denby said, "Reeves gives a

smashing physical performance as an action hero. Short-haired and bullet-headed, he offers a little personality—but not too much. There's a fascination in such hardball acting . . ."

Even *The New Yorker* had plenty of praise after taking time to go back and find fault with his performance in *Little Buddha*.

"Reeves makes an even better tough guy than you'd expect, and SWAT gear really suits him; he should wear it more often . . . Delivery isn't an issue here, because he doesn't have speeches—he doesn't have time for speeches. He has *lines*. In his muted way, Reeves is blessed with perfect pitch: aroused by the hazards thrown up by the plot, but not so smart that he forgets to be frightened by them; strong enough to carry the film, but never trying to swamp it with his presence."

Variety found fault with Keanu's lack of "expressive range," but was willing to concede that "he is appealingly, and surprisingly, forceful and commanding in the type of role he's never tackled before, and there's little doubt that this will bring him new audience identification and open up a new assortment of parts for him."

And *Rolling Stone* finally saw the light, saying, "Reeves is a major surprise; he cuts a sturdy figure . . . has the last laugh by delivering a vigorous, no bull performance that suggests we'll be able to hear his name in the future without silently mentioning the word 'dude.' "

Maybe they weren't all out unqualified raves about his work in the film, but compared to the way he'd been written about in the past, they might as well have been. As far as the writers were concerned, Keanu had arrived. Finally.

Just like the movie itself, the character of Jack Traven was a tweak of the action movie hero stereotype. He was a straight-down-the-line type of guy, a cop with a job to do, but unlike the action heros who'd preceded him in the cinema, he wasn't excessively macho. Quite the opposite. The bluff exterior concealed a personal shyness and a dry sense of humor. No flarings of emotion, no real gunplay. Jack was very human, a bit of an outsider. He wasn't the typical cop. With Annie he was solicitous rather than condescending in something vaguely approaching political correctness; the hero as a '90s man. To all intents and purposes, it redefined the concept of leading man for the genre.

The film also gave us a decidedly physical Keanu, biceps hard, ready to take on anything, anywhere, anytime.

"I didn't want to be *cut*," he told *People*, "but I

wanted to have somewhat of a beefy aspect to my chest and arms."

And he succeeded admirably; the weeks of intense weight training paid off. America has always had a soft spot for men of action, from John Wayne to Bruce Willis to Stephen Seagal. Even Sylvester Stallone has managed to keep his fans through a series of increasingly excruciating movies. As a rule, the acting ability needed hasn't been that great. And while this role didn't seem as if it was too much of a mental strain for Keanu, he was still able to offer quirks of character. His haircut, for example, was decidedly more functional than flattering, with nothing for a bad guy to grab onto, a clear indication that this was someone who was always thinking about his job. Yet Keanu remained close enough to the mainstream to make Jack Traven utterly compelling. Keanu had hit a home run.

Speed transformed him into a major star in the public's eyes. It was something that was bound to happen sooner or later. His acting ability and range had been evident for so long (even if the reviewers had kept denying it) that all he really needed was the right vehicle to give him mass exposure and make his name a household word. And now here he was, in something that was—quite literally—a runaway hit.

When he signed to play the SWAT cop, he'd been paid $1.2 million for his work. Curiously, the contract he signed didn't specify a salary for any possible sequel. Whether that was due to oversight or simply because the studio's expectations of *Speed* weren't high enough to consider another film in the series may never be known. But within a couple of months of the movie's release, *Speed 2* was becoming a very interesting concept to Twentieth Century Fox. They approached Keanu. Yes, he was interested, but he had a schedule that would carry him through the next eighteen months at least. To come back as Jack Traven he wanted $7 million. And full script approval. With barely a blink of an eye, the studio agreed. With that, there was no longer any doubt that Keanu had become a bona fide star.

It was about time, really. For eight years he'd been something of a workaholic, going directly from one project to the next, pushing himself as far as he could go, extending his range, challenging himself in film after film. He was a trained actor who'd continued to train, who wanted each performance to be better than the last and show something new. Over the course of seventeen films he'd attempted almost everything. If any actor deserved the big time, he did.

Nor was he the only one to emerge from *Speed*

with a greatly enhanced reputation. Sandra Bullock's bravura performance as Annie was noted with a great deal of interest. Once the movie opened, Sandra found herself inundated with scripts and offers, a leading lady at last.

Keanu already had as much work on his plate as he could handle. He was already signed to work until the end of 1995, first on the William Gibson cyberpunk thriller *Johnny Mnemonic*, where he would play the title role. After that would come *A Walk in the Clouds*, under the direction of Alfonso Arau, who made an artistic impact with *Like Water for Chocolate*. From there he'd go straight into *Feeling Minnesota* (whose title came from a song by Soundgarden), an independent film that would co-star rocker Courtney Love. Then, just to round out a very intense period of film work, Keanu would be in the thriller *Dead Drop*.

They were all very, very different. It was quite obvious that Keanu wasn't going to let his new star status alter the way he looked at acting. For him it was still about taking chances. Succeeding was always a triumph, but failure could be just fine, too.

And, as if all the movie work wasn't enough to keep him occupied, he made arrangements to return to what excited him about acting in the first place—live theater. Not just any play, but

Shakespeare, and the toughest role of all, the jewel in the crown—Hamlet.

Keanu was hardly a stranger to the Bard, of course. But this was really putting himself on the line and inviting comparison to some of the great performances of history—Sir Laurence Olivier, Ian MacKellen, and a number of others.

It all began with a phone call from Lewis Baumander, who'd directed the production of *Romeo and Juliet* that Keanu had been in as a teenager. The two had stayed in touch across the years, and now Baumander was working out in Winnipeg, Manitoba. Would Keanu be interested in playing Hamlet, Baumander wanted to know.

It was a tough decision to make. There was another offer in the pipeline for Keanu, an opportunity to work with Al Pacino and Robert De Niro, two of America's best actors, on a movie called *Heat*. But he'd always loved the theater, and Shakespeare. It was something he hadn't done in a long, long time. It would stretch him. After some reflection, he accepted the challenge.

At $2,000 a week, the money was chicken feed by movie standards. But this definitely wasn't about a salary. This was about art, satisfying himself, and proving something very important.

What no one involved with the project understood was just how popular Keanu had become. As soon as contracts had been exchanged in the summer of 1994, the production was announced. Immediately, the box office was filled with calls from all over the world. It was pure craziness; the theater in Winnipeg had never seen anything like it before.

By early December the city was already full of fans waiting for Keanu to arrive and begin rehearsals. The weather was painfully cold, but they'd clamor around the stage door for hours, hoping for a sight—or better yet, a sound—from their hero. The local paper, the *Winnipeg Free Press*, even began a Keanu Hotline, where people could record star sightings.

Exactly what they expected they didn't say—a long round of partying, perhaps, or Keanu strolling around the town. Whatever it was, they didn't get it. He quickly established a routine of going to the theater, then back to his hotel. Occasionally he'd eat in a restaurant. Word leaked out that he'd eaten at The Pocket Bar and Grill a couple of times, and suddenly the place was full of women hoping he might return.

Winnipeg was definitely flush with Keanu fever.

When he left a credit card in a clothing store at a local mall, the manager had him paged to retrieve it and a riot nearly ensued. It all seemed very strange to the locals, but overall they weren't complaining. Estimates translated this invasion into a $3.5 million boost to the economy, never a bad thing at the best of times, but in the dead of a bitter Canadian winter, it was scarcely believable.

The anticipation rose every day, as more and more visitors flocked into the city, coming from as far away as Finland, Australia, and Japan, filling the hotel rooms and phoning the box office in increasingly desperate attempts to secure tickets. But every show had been sold out for months. Given the Manitoba Theater Center's seating capacity of 789, and the limited run of 24 performances, from January 12 to February 4, 1995, a lot of people were likely to be disappointed. Even plenty of media representatives, anxious to be in on such a newsworthy story, found themselves ticketless.

Of course, there were ways to make sure you got a seat. The scalpers, out on the street, were having a field day, selling tickets with a face value of $36 for $750. They found no shortage of takers, people like Elke Schnell, who flew in from Germany without any promise of a ticket just to see Keanu.

And that was what it was all about—to really *see* him, in the flesh. Most of the crowds shivering around Winnipeg didn't care about Shakespeare. They were there for Keanu.

A cottage industry of sorts grew around souvenirs of the event. Particularly popular was a T-shirt (black, naturally) with Keanu's face on the front and a quote from the play—oddly enough, from a speech by Polonius, not Hamlet himself—"To thine own self be true."

The opening night was frantic. Television crews were set up in the theater lobby interviewing playgoers as they entered, then waiting for the verdict as they left. Backstage, the tension was high.

"Everyone was nervous except Keanu," Wayne Nicklas, who played Marcellus, remembered later. "He was the bravest of the cast, always leading the way."

Indeed, all through rehearsals Keanu had been relaxed. If the prospect of playing Hamlet and being compared to the real greats frightened him, he never showed it. Nor did he have the arrogance often associated with movie stars. He was just another member of the cast, perfectly friendly and charming with everyone else, not guarded, always ready to chat, and, above all, work hard.

Keanu had stated that he wanted to play "a Hamlet of passion and reason," but once the curtain rose on the first performance, had he succeeded? It was a daunting role, one which generally demanded years of training and experience to fully bring to life. Keanu had more formal training than most movie actors, but in stage terms he was still relatively unformed and undisciplined. And working on the stage was about as challenging as it was possible for acting to be. It meant playing the same part night after night with no second takes, no chances to cover up mistakes.

It was an daring move on Keanu's part, and his appearance may well have ended up generating more publicity than he'd expected or desired. But this wasn't publicity stunt or a gimmick of any kind. This was about seriously trying something. If he'd really wanted to make a splash, Keanu wouldn't have been portraying Hamlet in a relative backwater like Winnipeg, under the direction of one of his old college teachers. He'd have been doing it on Broadway, with his name in lights everywhere, working with internationally known talent.

Despite the difficulty of obtaining tickets, there were still plenty of critics in the theater that night. Even the London *Sunday Times* had sent a representative.

Perhaps understandably, Keanu came across as a little nervous on stage—it was his first time up there in almost ten years—speaking his lines quickly and losing some of the rhythm of the poetry. However, according to reports, he was excellent in the comic scenes, particularly those which required some action on his part. Throughout, though, he was very "earnest," but, as *Maclean's* reviewer Brian D. Johnson noted, "Even when his delivery was lacking, there was something intriguing about his presence. The ingenuous lilt to his voice, the blank sense of disconnection that he projects and his valiant efforts to overcome it—those qualities make him a more suitable casting choice for Hamlet than he might at first seem."

In the London *Sunday Times*, Roger Lewis surprisingly declared that he was "wonderful . . . He is one of the top three Hamlets I have seen for the simple reason: he is Hamlet. . . . He quite embodied the . . . undercurrents and overtones . . . that form the Prince of Denmark."

That was high praise indeed from such an august publication. But it certainly seemed that once Keanu became used to the footlights again, rather than the cameras, he became quite impressive. Some looked at his work a little more lightheartedly, like the Toronto *Globe and Mail*, which pointed out, "he does look great in tights." Nor was *The Ottawa Citizen* too harsh on him. The paper's critic concluded that "Reeves simply lacks the equipment for such a role," while *The Vancouver Sun* offered in faint praise, "He is never less than interesting onstage."

As might have been expected, really, the audience gave him a standing ovation. But whether his performance had truly been that wonderful or not, he deserved it just for the courage he'd shown in being willing to undertake such a venture, for placing art above the millions he could have been making in Hollywood.

Once he'd removed his makeup he attended the post-show reception, where he was naturally cornered by fans, mostly (and hardly surprisingly) young women who wanted his autograph. For someone still going through the adrenaline surge that follows such a draining activity, he was remarkably kind and patient, spending half an hour with them, then more time later on, doing exactly the same thing for those waiting outside the stage door.

Then run continued smoothly, playing to capacity crowds every night. Keanu, as director Baumander described him, was not "your retiring, wimpy Hamlet." Indecision and confusion was an inherent part of the character, but once Hamlet's decision had been made towards the end of the play, Keanu showed the audience a man in command, athletic in the final fight scene and somewhat glorious as well as tragic, in death.

Many had expected him to fall flat on his face when confronted with the classic play, but Keanu carried himself very, very well. Perhaps it wasn't an artistic triumph on a par with the towering stage names, but it nonetheless showed that he had resources still untapped by the movies, areas inside himself himself that he wanted to explore—and that he was finally ready to look at.

The praise he'd been given also left the door open for future stage work. If the critics had savaged him, as might almost have been anticipated, given that he didn't come from the "pure" background of stage work, then that might have been an end to it. But this way, encouraged, it remained quite feasible that he would undertake some other dark role sometime, at least when his demanding film schedule allowed. And with his ongoing love of Shakespeare, it's not impossible that in the future we could see him in *Macbeth*, or even in some of the comedies—Keanu has, after all, shown a natural talent for the comic throughout his career.

For now, though, with the satisfaction of Winnipeg behind him, it was time to return to what for him had become the real world—making movies.

CHAPTER ELEVEN

It was chance that brought Keanu into *Johnny Mnemonic*, the film made from William Gibson's short story. Val Kilmer had originally been set to play the title role, starring above punk rock icon Henry Rollins, rapper Ice-T, and Japanese actor Takeshi Kitano. Everything was in place. In fact, pre-production work was already underway in Toronto when Kilmer left the project for reasons that have still never been fully detailed.

It was enough to put everything on the edge of disaster. Work shut down for a month, although producer B.J. Rack and director Robert Longo remained in Canada, trying to hold things together. They needed a new lead, and they needed to re-arrange their financing.

Keanu received the script in a roundabout way, not through his agent. "It arrived on my doorstep," he said. "It was given to me by a friend of a friend."

Speed hadn't yet appeared in theaters; indeed, the filming was barely over, so Keanu hadn't yet become a megastar. That meant Longo was able to secure his services for much less than he'd have had to pay a few months later. For Keanu it meant that once again he was completing one movie and heading straight into another, not getting the break he really needed.

Luckily, the shoot was quick. But at the same time it was very intense. Keanu was featured in almost every scene. Towards the end he could feel just how drained he was becoming.

"I was trying not to move so that I could save my strength," he recalled.

With a great deal of publicity—including a MTV special on Keanu that featured an interview with him—*Johnny Mnemonic* opened in theaters on Memorial Day weekend in 1995.

To those familiar with the world Gibson had created in his books, this was familiar territory. We were in the twenty-first century. Everything was controlled by corporations who used the Yakuza, the Japanese Mafia, as their enforcers. The haves lived very well. Those who chose to opt out of the system, or were forced out, were called the LoTeks and scratched a living out the decaying inner cities. And there was a new plague loose in the world, NAS (Nerve Attenuation Syndrome), which caused the debilitating "black shakes," that ultimate end was death.

Johnny (Keanu) was a mnemonic courier, someone who had an implant in his brain that allowed him to upload and transport data. Essentially, he was a smuggler, his services available for a hefty price to whoever could afford them.

But he wanted his own memories back. That meant an expensive operation. So Johnny was on one last run, overloading his capacity.

From the start there was something wrong. What should have been straightforward turned into a series of catastrophes, and Johnny ended up in Newark with the Yakuza on his tail. The only person willing to help him—for money—was Janie (Dina Meyer), a woman with enhanced strength who wanted to be a bodyguard.

They were on the run, in the city and in cyberspace, trying to keep one jump ahead of the Yakuza and the man they'd hired, a killer known as the Preacher. Aid came from the LoTeks, under the leadership of J-Bone (Ice-T), who took Johnny and

Janie into their headquarters, finally holding off an assault from the Yakuza as they broadcast the information Johnny had been carrying—the cure for NAS.

It was an elaborate production that didn't stint on special effects, including a wonderful virtual reality trip through the Internet. Director Robert Longo might have taken a little inspiration from both *Blade Runner* and *Mad Max*, but what he ended up with was something entirely new, a world polished to a sheen on one side, rough as old stone on the other. It was also glorious entertainment. *Johnny Mnemonic* offered plenty of stunts, action, and violence. But when it came down to it, was the picture just a variation on the shoot 'em up James Bond formula, or did it have something more to offer? Was it a B-movie with a big name star?

At its heart, it was an action movie every bit as much as *Speed*. The difference was that the hero here was more passive. He could move, he could fight, but he remained a pawn. He was not in control of his own life. Greedy, pampered, he was suddenly in a situation he couldn't handle. He had to rely on others for the first time, and was distrustful of good intentions, being unsure of having any himself. Through happenstance he was swept up into events.

At least the film didn't take itself too seriously. The drama and action was lightened by moments of comedy and gentle parody—Ralphie's slimy Peter Lorre characterization, Johnny's petulant outburst under the bridge, yelling "I want room service!" (a speech actually suggested by Keanu, then scripted by Gibson). And at the end, there was a spoof on the action device of the bad guy returning to life. The Preacher moved, only for a camera pan back to reveal his corpse being hauled by a crane. For dealing with a hero who wanted to be mostly a machine, the movie was surprisingly human. But then again, that was the state Johnny wanted to return to.

It's doubtful that Val Kilmer could have brought as much to the role of Johnny as Keanu did. He was truly able to humanize Johnny, to put a heart inside the sharp suit, and alter the pace between drama and humor without missing a beat. For someone who came into the project completely drained, it was a miraculous performance of angst and action. Even more so, according to Gibson (who also wrote the screenplay), since after reading the script, Keanu asked, "What's he want? I don't get this guy?"

His strong fan base among the teens and twentysomethings also made Keanu a perfect fit for this film. With its high tech, cyberpunk outlook, those were exactly the age groups it was aiming at. Add to that the legion of people who'd loved Keanu in *Speed* and you had a potential blockbuster, a summer blast almost as perfect as the last one.

Dina Meyer, in her film debut after work in television, was also impressive as the woman who, if not of steel, was of more than flesh and blood. There was real chemistry between her and Keanu, although she could never quite grasp what he was thinking.

"He's very quiet, very introverted," she told *People*. "You look at him, and you can see the wheels are turning, but you can't figure him out—if he's happy, if he's sad . . . you just want to say 'What's happening in there?' "

What was happening, of course, was that Keanu was becoming Johnny, the way he became all his characters. That was his way, his Method. And he made it work superbly.

At least his fans thought so. The majority of the population seemed unmoved to see the film, which didn't prove to be the summer blockbuster that the studio had hoped. It opened reasonably well, but never made the type of money that seemed likely to break records. After a few weeks, its performance largely faded away.

Much of that could, perhaps, be traced to the reviews—at least, to those that made it into print. *Johnny Mnemonic* seemed, for some strange reason, largely avoided by the press. And when the spotlight did shine on it, the judgments weren't kind. *People* announced, "*Johnny Mnemonic* . . . is a violent jumble," while *Entertainment Weekly* called it "a slack and derivative future-shock thriller." And *Maclean's*, which might have been sympathetic to a production largely filmed in Canada and starring a Canadian, offered the harshest call of all, saying that "Cyberpunk has given birth to cyberschlock."

The magazines didn't spare Keanu, either, choosing—unfairly—to relate Johnny's blank slate to Keanu's own personality. "Keanu Reeves wears a clean-cut science fiction hairdo that brings out the finely chiseled blankness of his features," was *Entertainment Weekly's* comment—and that was one of the less sniggering asides in the press.

But most who paid money to see it truly enjoyed the film, both as a piece of work in itself, and for Keanu's performance, which was much better than the reviewers made it out to be.

It might not have been a hit, yet in the long run *Johnny Mnemonic* added to the foundation of his stardom. In some ways, perhaps, it was almost a blessing for his career that it didn't do too well at the box office. As his first release after *Speed*, it could have left him stereotyped again, this time as the quirky hero of action films.

As it was, though, he wasn't about to be tied down so easily. With no real break after filming, he headed back to L.A. from the locations in Toronto and Montreal to start work on *A Walk In The Clouds*. He needed a change, and this was going to be it. He was moving from action hero to romantic lead.

CHAPTER TWELVE

The unexpected success of *Like Water For Chocolate* had brought director Alfonso Arau to the attention of Hollywood. He became, as they say, a hot property. He was wooed by the studios, all eager to tap into the special kind of magic he seemed to be able to produce on celluloid.

He knew the type of film he wanted to make— something lush and romantic—the sort of movie that had been popular in America half a century ago, but which had gone out of fashion in the high-tech consciousness of the '90s.

More than that, he knew who he wanted for the male lead—Keanu Reeves. In Arau's opinion, Keanu had never played a role which showed him fully as a man, a rounded person with both problems and passion.

"I said," Arau recalled in *Vanity Fair*, " 'Keanu, you are going to have to interpret as a grown man, as opposed to an adolescent.' "

It was an opportunity for Keanu to try something different, to take something he'd touched on in *Tune In Tomorrow* and build on it. Intrigued both by Arau's work and his proposal, he committed himself to play the returning war veteran in the film.

But working with Arau wasn't just a case of rehearsing and shooting the scenes. Like Keanu, Arau was a perfectionist. Acting alone wasn't enough. He wanted his performers to become the people they portrayed, something which meshed completely with Keanu's ideals.

"In rehearsals, we did some improvs," Keanu explained. "Alfonso and I concocted a situation where I lost a buddy, so I'd have that in my body . . . I wanted to have a man who through his experiences had come back desperately lonely, had seen death, and that caused in him an appreciation for life."

While the film was something of a departure from the work Keanu had done recently, it was just another facet of his personality.

Keanu was Paul Sutton, just back from harrowing years in World War II to his San Francisco home, where he thought his wife might be waiting on the quay to meet him. But she wasn't.

They'd married after one night together, and she was the closest thing to a family that Paul, an orphan, had. Not that she seemed to care.

Paul resumed his old job as a chocolate salesman; it would offer a breathing space while he figured out what to do with his life. On the train to Sacramaneto he literally bumped into a woman, then met her again on a bus, where he stopped two men from bothering her, and was ejected for his troubles.

The woman was Victoria Aragon (Aitana Sanchez-Gijon), and he encountered her for a third time, sitting by the road, crying. She was on her way home to tell her winemaker father that she was pregnant. And single.

Paul had a solution of sorts. He offered to pose as her husband, then sneak out the following morning, "abandoning" her.

It seemed like a good idea. But when he attempted to leave, he was waylaid by the family, and persuaded to stay. And then he fell in love with Victoria. However, he thought that she didn't care for him, and returned to San Francisco, only to discover that his legal wife had obtained a divorce.

He returned to the Aragons' vineyard, to ask for Victoria's hand. In a fight with her father, a fire began, which burned acres of grapes. Only the original vine remained. Amazingly, it was still alive. Planted, everything could begin again. And Paul was welcomed into the family.

It was melodrama of a kind that Hollywood hadn't attempted in many years—sweeping, romantic, sometimes even sappy. But in an era when the commercial cinema was dominated by thrillers and high tech violence (and Keanu had played in his share of those), it came as a very refreshing change of pace. Never mind some of the illogical twists of the script; the overall feel contained much of a sense of magic. Not the "magic realism" that pervaded South American literature and that director Arau had incorporated into *Like Water For Chocolate*, but the spell of a wonderful place, a special family, and a remarkable love.

As Paul Sutton, Keanu brought an openness and honesty to the role. Paul wasn't a complex man. During the war he'd had time to reflect on what he wanted from his life. Things could be boiled down to one word—happiness. At that was something his marriage couldn't offer, but Victoria could.

After the closed-off characters of Jack Traven and Johnny Mnemonic, Paul was a real breath of fresh air, a true challenge for an actor. Which made Keanu the perfect person for the role. And, in a curious way, the period when the film was set— 1945—truly suited him. The clothes flattered him, particularly the uniform, and the soft cut of his hair emphasized something that hadn't really been apparent before—that Keanu had classic movie idol looks. His smile seemed warm and genuine, not that of an actor, but a human being.

His main following had always been young women, perhaps not too surprisingly since he'd tended to play younger parts. But this, if anything could, and would, show him as attractive to a much wider range of people. He was still playing a man who was fairly young, but his character was a timeless one who, in an earlier age, could just as easily have been played by either Jimmy Stewart or Clark Gable.

The reviewers, sadly, seemed to have mixed opinions about the movie, and about Keanu's performance in it. *Maclean's* found it to be "over-fermented with symbols of the vineyard as the root of family values," which seemed to overlook the fact that the winery *was* the basis of the Aragon family life. The critic also felt that the dialogue was full of "romance novel cliches." There might have been a little truth in that, but not in any bad way.

People *do* speak in cliches; they're a kind of short-hand. And, certainly, in the context, it didn't seem ridiculous or embarrassing.

As for Keanu's portrayal of Paul, the magazine was happy to discover that he was "surprisingly adept," and that he displayed "a poise that he has not shown before."

That remark was much kinder than *People*, which, while admitting he was "handsome and hunky," thought his "dogged earnestness" just wasn't enough.

As for the movie itself, critic Leah Rozen did seem to like the fact that it was "swooningly romantic," but in the end decided that it "never achieves the kind of lightfootedness its title promises and its far-fetched story needs."

At least *Time*'s reviewer enjoyed the film, finding in it "a kind of romantic grandeur" with "something inspiring." The writer did see something of the tradition of magic realism in the "playful fate" that seemed to decree Paul and Victoria should be together, and even found a word of praise for Aitana Sanchez-Gijon's work, calling her character "meltingly portrayed."

However, there was little mention of Keanu's work; the review focused more on what Arau had achieved with the movie, which was "slicker and neater" than *Like Water for Chocolate*, but "just as irritating."

The range of comments left casual readers not quite sure what to think. But it certainly didn't keep audiences away. The film opened very strongly at the box office, and, if its success continued, seemed to ensure a return to the Hollywood traditions of yesteryear.

Keanu, though, had long since moved on to his next project, the independent production *Feeling Minnesota*, which was filmed in the Twin Cities. It was a sort of film noir that would show him in yet another, darker light, and open up another facet of his abilities, that wouldn't make the overall picture any clearer, just more enigmatic.

CHAPTER THIRTEEN

Keanu Reeves has become one of the biggest names in Hollywood. That's beyond question. But he may well be one of the unlikeliest stars there. He certainly hasn't followed the traditional path to fame, but virtually the opposite, really. He's not a standard issue hunk. Even his face isn't conventionally handsome like, say, Brad Pitt, but is more intriguing, more mysterious. And he's managed it all despite the stereotype of the role that established him—Ted Logan, of course—by the sheer range and versatility of his acting.

It's never been purely an ego thing for him. He's one of the few who's been more than willing to take small supporting roles when his stature could have given him something more. But ever since he first discovered it, and what it did for him, acting has been the center of his life.

Acting—*not* being a star. He eschews all the regular trappings of success, the big house in the Hollywood Hills, the limos and expensive lunches.

He has said that, "As long as it doesn't have to be about money, then it's *not* about money." It's art.

He's claimed that someday he wants to settle down, but that time seems to be a long way off. For the moment he's perfectly content with his relatively spartan life in hotel rooms, a life with very few possessions and his beloved Norton for tranportation.

"I'm a very private person," he told *Seventeen*. ". . . I'm a person who doesn't want too much."

It's a pared down life. A true actor's life.

Maybe his stardom was inevitable—after *Point Break* it was just waiting to be acknowledged and exploited, really—but it was never a goal in and of itself. What the increased visibility and power gave Keanu that he cared about was the freedom to pursue the roles he truly desired, to extend his reach, to succeed—or to fail. Of course, the successes far outnumbered the failures. That's something he'll almost certainly ensure he's able to keep doing, even as a major figure. And though the stakes have risen these days, and he can't afford to take all the chances and walk the tightrope the way he could when he wasn't such a public figure, Keanu isn't someone who'll ever be happy playing it safe.

Acting remains the complete focus of his life, with music a distant second. He worked incredibly hard, moving from one film to the next at a pace that would exhaust most actors, hiding himself in roles like a chameleon. Where can he go from here?

Even he doesn't seem to know. Keanu has no career plan.

"I have no idea," he said when *Speed* was released. "I certainly don't want to be an action hero. I don't even want a crystal ball."

But even if he ends up associated with Jack Traven for a while, it's at least better than the years he endured being associated with Ted Logan, and all those "excellent" and "dude" jokes in reviews. They evaporated over time (although a few persist, even today). The link with Traven will dissipate too.

Perhaps the greatest advantage Keanu's fame has given him is control, the ability to ensure that the movies he's in are quality products. For *Speed 2* he demanded script approval—if it was to be made he didn't want some tacky knock-off of the original. That was simply a matter of pride. But now he has absolutely no financial need to be involved with anything that's less than great. He already has a development deal to help him bring ideas he likes to fruition.

And though big-budget features will continue to be his stock in trade, you can be sure he won't completely turn his back on small films. *Feeling Minnesota* is an independent movie. He's made them before, and when it's feasible he'll almost certainly make them again. He's searching for the best projects, the ones where he can do something different. If they're challenging, it doesn't really matter if they can't pay $7 million. He already has more money than he can ever use. Other than for some negotiations, it's stopped being a factor. All the money means is that he can afford some of the "older Bordeaux" vintage wines he loves.

If you will, it's the slacker ethic in action, interest over cash. In other words, art stays at the front of his mind.

Given that, it's quite probable that he'll do more theatrical work in the future. Far more than movies, that's where his greatest challenge seems to lie—in creating a role night after night. And stage work is the foundation of his acting experience; it's his home. After *Hamlet* was received well, a performance that was something of an experiment, testing the waters, the idea has to have stayed in his mind.

Nor is his involvement in Dogstar likely to vanish any time soon. It remains strictly his side project, a release, a safety valve for his personality. Just as importantly, it's his chance to be involved with music, which has always been a vital part of his life. He needs it. He has a pretty fair assessment of the band, which one record industry insider described as "totally awful," but whether they're good or bad doesn't matter. The band exists. It satisfies another of his needs. In the summer of 1994, the band undertook a succesful club tour, selling out a string of dates. However, there's no doubt that the majority of people weren't there to hear the music, but to see Keanu at close range.

And while Dogstar would never be a full-time occupation for him, Keanu did announce that the band had plans to record an album. An album would be a better acid test than any live performance, allowing the band to be judged on its musical, rather than visual, merits.

Director Gus Van Sant once characterized Keanu as "sort of a punk rocker, in a way," which is true, and more than just in a musical way. He came of age in an unconventional household when punk was still on the fringes. It was the music of outsiders, of rebellion. It was *his* music—he went to see the bands, he bought their albums. He identified with it, and he's never stopped doing so. Appearing on a movie set in a skirt and combat boots might have been "comfortable" (and possibly ridiculous), but it was also completely punk.

In its original incarnation, punk was a rejection of a society that didn't speak to the young. It was a step outside society, and to a point, that's where Keanu has stayed ever since, with his refusal to acquire the usual trappings of stardom. And outsiders are the people he's always related to in his acting, whether as Siddhartha, Hamlet, or even as Marty in *Tune in Tomorrow*, who walks away from the life laid out for him to follow his heart.

He's even portrayed the ultimate American rebel—James Dean—recreating some of the scenes from *Rebel Without A Cause* for the video of Paula Abdul's song "Rush, Rush," which left him saying, "... James Dean was like, wow. I knew I could never do his gig."

Dean was an enigma; so is Keanu. It's not deliberate, or any kind of manufactured image. He simply seems uncomfortable in public situations. Interviewers have found him somewhat reticent and tongue-tied, inarticulate about his feelings and idiosyncratic to the point of eccentricity when he walks away to consider answers and talks to himself (although a televised interview on MTV found him relaxed, loquacious, and charming). That kind of behavior has even led some people to wonder about his intelligence.

That just stands as an odd, sad commentary on the way we expect our stars and celebrities to behave. We seem to want them to be outgoing, always ready with a sound bite, and ultimately more normal than any of us.

There's certainly no reason for them to be that way. The actors we pay to watch at larger than life size are playing someone else, not themselves. So, if Keanu isn't exceptionally gregarious and articulate in interviews, does it matter? His fame is as an actor. His eloquence comes from the words other people write. As long as he can make us believe the person on screen or on stage is real, he's succeeded. He doesn't need—and obviously doesn't want—to be a celebrity in his own right.

And it certainly doesn't offer any grounds for believing him to be lacking in intelligence.

"Keanu is really well-read, but he doesn't think he is," was Gus Van Sant's comment. And, indeed, Keanu's read his way through Shakespeare, Dostoevski, Thomas Mann, and even Stephen Hawking—hardly the material for someone supposedly lacking in brainpower.

As to his other quirks—are they really important? In a way, they serve to make him more all the more endearing, and far more human than the usual Hollywood actor. He always has been, and probably always will be, very much of an individual, not merely another good-looking face out of the same mold.

Though he'd rather be acclaimed for his acting, the truth is that much of the basis for Keanu's popularity is the way he looks, and the smoldering charisma he portrays on the camera. In 1995, *People* picked him as one of the "50 Most Beautiful People." He has an appeal to both sexes. Women find him attractive, not so much for his masculinity as the vulnerability he exudes; there's nothing threatening or overly macho about him. The temptation is to mother him as much as make love to him. He seems approachable, not on any kind of pedestal. And for men he's someone they could easily imagine themselves being—the stretch really doesn't seem *that* great; he has something of the regular guy in him.

That appeal even extends to the gay community. From his first professional appearance in Toronto, in the play *Wolftrap*, Keanu has always enjoyed a gay following. That, not unnaturally, increased with *My Own Private Idaho*, a movie that triggered rumors that he was gay himself—rumors he tried to squash by explicity stating his heterosexuality.

But on one level or another, the rumors continued intermittently, aided by the fact that he's had no real girlfriend or relationship of any kind, preferring to squire around different women—"your blonde flavor of the week" as one friend called the procession of females.

In 1995, everything came to a head when a French magazine recorded in print that Keanu and a movie producer had undergone a gay wedding ceremony. And while it was never given much credence by the American press, it was too good a rumor not to be repeated. Until Keanu's publicist, Robert Garlock, issued a statement reaffirming that Keanu was not gay, and that he and David Geffen had never even met, let alone married.

"It's so ridiculous," Keanu told *Vanity Fair* later, "I find it funny," adding, "... there's nothing wrong with being gay, so to deny it is to make a judgment. And why make a big deal of it? If someone doesn't want to hire me because they think I'm gay, well, then I have to deal with it, I guess. Or if people were picketing a theater. But otherwise, it's just gossip, isn't it?"

And Geffen, too, scotched the rumors, saying, "I hear that I'm supposed to be married to Keanu Reeves. I've never met or laid eyes on [him]." Will that be the end of things? Maybe, but undoubtedly some kind of talk will persist until the time Keanu eventually meets a woman and settles down.

He has said that sometime, eventually, he'd like to marry and become a father. For the immediate future, though, it seems unlikely. He seems to have consciously steered away from relationships and commitments—to an extent, he feels, because of his father and mother separating when he was young. "I think a lot of who I am is a reaction against his actions."

It could also explain what he calls his "gypsy-bohemian philosophy" of "I don't want a home because I don't want roots." (While he owns no home in Los Angeles, he does have an apartment on New York's Upper East Side). As long as he's working, moving from one activity to another, be it acting, music, or whatever, that's something he doesn't have to think about. But it will, however, change eventually. It won't be a case of "growing up" or "becoming responsible," but simply the desire for change and a chance to slow down to look at his life and see what he wants to do with it, where he'd like it to go.

That he'll endure and gain in stature as an actor seems beyond question. He's grown so much in the nine years since his appearance in *River's Edge*, and worked at his craft so incessantly. Very little seems out of bounds to him. It's quite within reason that he could go on to become one of the great movie actors, on a par with Paul Newman, one of the few who seems able to combine art with style and box office success. Keanu has the ability and he has the desire. All it will take is time.

At some point he may even try his hand at directing—it seems a common enough step for actors to take. But portrayal of characters will always remain his long suit, the gift he's been given.

All that assumes, of course, that he doesn't have some fatal crash on his Norton. As it is, the scars increase. Riding a motorcycle—particularly in Los Angeles traffic—becomes more dangerous every day. And the late night rides, when "I'll just go out, say, around one. Midnight. And I'll ride until four. Goin' through the city to see who's doin' what where, you know?" contain their own problems. But, as he's said, "I love that bike, man."

He's a gentle survivor. When River Phoenix died he experienced the pain of loss. It was a very sobering shock. And he has something to live for—

acting. The most difficult times are when he's not doing it.

"Once you get a part, you're liberated," he once said. It's the drive inside that keeps him doing it, something over which he has no choice.

"I've always cared about acting," he told *US*. And the care has paid off. The work he's thrown himself into headlong has pitched him up on the beach smiling. He keeps surprising us with the range of his ability, from goofy teenager to action hero to romantic lead. And he's not likely to stop— at least, not for many years yet.

The victim is found facedown in a plate of spaghetti. It's the first in a series of unspeakable crimes so depraved and twisted that even veteran city cops can't look at them. And each murder comes with a name: this one is gluttony.

Somerset doesn't want this case. The city's best homicide cop, he's just one week from retiring—a week he planned to spend training his replacement David Mills, a real pain-in-the-butt go-getter. But after the second murder, Somerset knows there's a madman out there, one promising to avenge all seven deadly sins—and only he and Mills can stop him....

SEVEN

**THE ELECTRIFYING NOVEL
BY ANTHONY BRUNO—
BASED ON THE BLOCKBUSTER MOTION PICTURE
STARRING BRAD PITT AND MORGAN FREEMAN**

SEVEN
Anthony Bruno
_____ 95704-1 $4.99 U.S./$5.99 CAN.

They were called the class from Hell—thirty-four inner-city sophomores she inherited from a teacher who'd been "pushed over the edge." She was told "those kids have tasted blood. They're dangerous."

But LouAnne Johnson had a different idea. Where the school system saw thirty-four unreachable kids, she saw young men and women with intelligence and dreams. When others gave up on them, she broke the rules to give them the best things a teacher can give— hope and belief in themselves. When statistics showed the chances were they'd never graduate, she fought to beat the odds.

This is her remarkable true story—and theirs.

DANGEROUS MINDS

LOUANNE JOHNSON

NOW A MAJOR MOTION PICTURE FROM HOLLYWOOD PICTURES STARRING

MICHELLE PFEIFFER

He's already blown up a subway. He's already sent the NYPD scrambling. Now, he's holding the entire city of New York hostage with the world's deadliest explosive—and he's making John McClane jump through hoops.

Once McClane was the best. Then he lost everything. Now, he's racing against the clock, following orders from a psycho bomber who's made massive destruction into a very personal game of revenge: when the city goes up, McClane will die first.

It can't happen. It won't happen. With a tough, streetwise partner, John McClane races across a panicked city, smashing the rules, locked and loaded for the ultimate duel...

DIE HARD
WITH A VENGEANCE

A novel by D. Chiel
Based on a screenplay written by Jonathan Hensleigh
Now a major motion picture
Starring Bruce Willis, Jeremy Irons and Samuel L. Jackson
and Directed by John McTiernan

_____ 95676-2 $4.99 U.S./$5.99 Can.

Sheer genius had earned Eddie Gold a role
among the government's covert elite—inventing
high-tech gadgets of mayhem that he thought
would be useful in the fight for freedom abroad.

But someone has used one of his creations
to murder a Washington power broker. Now
there's innocent blood on his hands, and justice
on his mind. And when he begins to dig
for answers, his superiors suddenly
become his deadliest enemies.

CHAIN REACTION

THE NOVEL BY ROBERT TINE—

BASED ON THE BLOCKBUSTER ACTION THRILLER
STARRING KEANU REEVES AND MORGAN FREEMAN